Praise for *Swipe*

"*Swipe* takes a deep look into the science and psychology of distraction, attention, and disengagement, giving us the tools we need to focus on and finish what's most important. I truly love this book!"

Paul B. Allen, co-founder of Ancestry.com, CEO of Soar.com

"Research clearly shows that self-aware people are more successful and promotable, yet few find the time to invest in this essential skill—instead, we fall victim to what the authors smartly call the 'Swipe.' This book will help you find the power to stop reacting and start acting."

Dr. Tasha Eurich, organizational psychologist and *New York Times* bestselling author of *Insight* and *Bankable Leadership*

"I have learned in my leadership roles that engagement and culture drive success. But as *Swipe* clearly illustrates, we quickly become distracted. This book is an invaluable guide for putting aside distraction in order to achieve both personal and organizational results."

Jeremy Andrus, CEO, Traeger Grills

"Technology has reshaped every aspect of our lives, including the way we think. When the distractions of life, often brought on by the world of technology, cause us to disengage and 'check out,' *Swipe* shows us how to get things done."

Jason Ward, executive vice president of people and customers, Azul Airlines, Brazil

SWIPE

an imprint of Amplify Publishing Group

www.amplifypublishinggroup.com

Swipe: The Science Behind Why We Don't Finish What We Start

For more information, please contact:
Amplify Publishing, an imprint of Amplify Publishing Group
620 Herndon Parkway, Suite 320
Herndon, VA 20170
info@amplifypublishing.com

Library of Congress Control Number: 2022912960

CPSIA Code: PRV0922A

ISBN-13: 978-1-64543-553-2

Printed in the United States

To our families, friends, and colleagues—
our reasons for not Swiping.

SWIPE

The Science Behind Why
We Don't Finish What We Start

Tracy Maylett

Tim Vandehey

an imprint of Amplify Publishing Group

Contents

Introduction 3

CHAPTER 1   The Graveyard of Abandoned Dreams 15

CHAPTER 2   Swipeland 33

CHAPTER 3   The Human Cost of the Swipe 53

CHAPTER 4   Disengaged: The Swipe at Work.......................73

CHAPTER 5   The Hamster Wheel 101

CHAPTER 6   There's an App for That....................................119

CHAPTER 7   The Psychology of the Swipe...........................137

CHAPTER 8   The Swipe and the Brain 161

CHAPTER 9   Master Your Attention 183

CHAPTER 10   Escaping the Hamster Wheel 201

Endnotes 229

About the Authors...243

Index 245

Introduction

> Swiping is the mental act of reflexively dismissing an uncomfortable or disturbing present in the hope that something better and easier is just around the corner.

Chris Baty wasn't a frustrated novelist, but back in 1999 he was curious about something. Could he and a bunch of wannabe, sort-of authors each complete a fifty-thousand-word fiction manuscript—the length of a typical novel—in just thirty days if quality was not an issue? He had no idea, but it sounded like fun, so he and twenty-one friends in the San Francisco Bay Area took the pledge and wrote their hearts out. The only rules: the work had to be new, only one person could write it, and it had to be over fifty thousand words by midnight on November 30. The next year, 140 intrepid writers took their shot, and National Novel Writing Month, or NaNoWriMo, was born.

"We had the classic NaNoWriMo experience, which I think a lot of people have on their first time, where it was wildly underplanned," Baty says. "There was no outlining, no character notes, and the story just kind of took shape. I thought, 'If I can do this, anybody can do this.' It was an epiphany."

Since that beginning, millions of aspiring authors have found reasons to try NaNoWriMo, hunkering down alone and in groups, with laptops, notes, and lots of caffeine, every November 1 to try to bang out a work of long fiction. Baty's experiment has blossomed into a good-natured cottage industry. In 2020 more than 552,000 writers from six continents officially participated in NaNoWriMo, and the challenge has spawned a Young Writers Program, Camp NaNoWriMo, partnerships with libraries and bookstores, and more. And while the quality of the finished work is incidental—the point for most participants is just to finish, not to win—a handful of NaNoWriMo novels have been published to great acclaim, including Sara Gruen's *Water for Elephants*, Erin Morgenstern's *The Night Circus*, Hugh Howey's *Wool*, Rainbow Rowell's *Fangirl*, Jason Hough's *The Darwin Elevator*, and Marissa Meyer's *Cinder*.

As Baty points out, what's made NaNoWriMo a phenomenon is that it helps frustrated novelists *finally* finish something after years of false starts—or even just to begin writing at all. "When it comes to creative projects, there are a million good reasons to not do it," he says. "When I started it, I didn't come at it from a position of a frustrated novelist. I had no doubts about having written a book, because I hadn't tried it before. So I think when it started, the goal was really just getting a feasible draft out in a short amount of time. It was great for that. The thing that surprised me was that the idea of lowering the bar to just *completion*—the big completion of a crappy first draft—really helped people turn off that perfectionist voice that a lot of us have."

An international movement built on the promise of giving people the structure and motivation to finish something after a lifetime of frustrating failures. We couldn't come up with a more perfect analog for this book if we tried.

Babies Do It, Teens Do It, Even Celebs in Magazines Do It

Flick.

Pinch.

Reverse pinch.

Swipe.

Each of those words describes one of the common gestures we use to command capacitive touch screens, those magical sheets of glass that let us do what we want with our smartphones and tablets. But that's still not what we're going to talk about—not yet. We're here to talk about how we choose what to explore in our world—specifically, how babies do it.

Psychology researchers have found that infants as young as seventeen days old will make swiping movements with their hands and arms toward nearby objects they find visually interesting, and that this action appears naturally "preprogrammed."[1] They've also observed that babies who reach for objects rather than just looking at them also seem better able to connect an action and a goal.[2] Swiping seems to be a primitive, natural way of managing our environment that brings us pleasure and helps us curate our experiences. It's no wonder app and user interface (UX) designers decided to make the swipe gesture an integral part of navigating their products.

Swiping is such a natural motion for humans that Google's Material Design system defines it as distinct from scrolling or flicking. Because swiping is like sliding a card off the top of the deck in blackjack or Texas Hold'em—Google describes the movement as "slid(ing) elements to complete actions upon passing a threshold"[3]—it satisfies our natural impulse to progress to the next thing, and then the next, and the next. The movement also mimics the way we read in many of the world's languages—left to right but also right to left as we relocate our gaze to the beginning of the next line.

More importantly, swiping satisfies the universal craving for novelty. When you scroll your phone's screen or pinch a photo on Google Maps, you're experiencing a different aspect of the same material—a different way of viewing what's already in front of you. However, when you swipe in the Tinder app, to a new screen on your iPhone, or to a new page in a book, you're leaving your present experience behind and moving toward something fresh and unpredictable. The allure of the next new thing, not to mention our anticipation of it, tickles the brain's reward pathways, as Richard Pallardy writes on App Partner:

> Apps like Tinder employ what is called a "variable reward schedule," much like a slot machine at a casino. Each rejected card in the stack builds anticipation in the user, who expects that eventually, something good will come along—say, a prospective date. This process harnesses the brain's reward pathway, releasing dopamine. This same chemical is released by a wide range of activities, including eating and using drugs. Intriguingly, dopamine is also released by the anticipation of the reward, often at higher levels than are released by the consumption of the reward itself.[4]

That's one reason swipe-based dating apps, like Tinder and Bumble, are so popular. Just leafing through them, searching for your soul mate, feels good. Swiping turns out to be a nifty tool for a little friendly psychological manipulation.

The One That Got Away and Other Small Tragedies

When we swipe on our phones, we're choosing to disengage. We've elected to change our digital environment because we're bored, confused, or uncomfortable with what is in front of us. In the real world, we do the same thing. When we Swipe—note the capitalization—we choose to disengage with something or someone. That something or someone might be trivial, a momentary irritant with no consequence. No problem.

On the other hand, it could be someone or something asking us to bring our hearts, spirits, minds, and hands to the moment, and we say, "I'd rather not," as we sprint out the door. Innocuous? Maybe. Until it isn't. Swiping is reflexive; unconscious; and sometimes done at a time of annoyance, discomfort, or even panic. It's not as though we're considering the evidence and making a rational decision when we decide to discard the present and move on to whatever's next. It's the psychological equivalent of seeing a wasp in your peripheral vision and instantly ducking away while swatting wildly at the air.

That means swiping—or, as we'll call it from here on, the Swipe—can easily have unintended consequences. For instance, do you have a lost love in your past, someone you broke up with because things were getting too serious? Many do, and they regard those affairs with no small measure of wistful regret. Did they pass up the love of their lives? They'll never know, which is what makes such entanglements so painful. (Ironically, Tinder and Bumble have addressed this in their apps, creating a feature that lets users go back and revisit past swipes. They realized that people often swipe quickly and later regret what might have been.)

What about leaving a job or disengaging in our work when it gets too challenging, or ceases to be challenging enough? We're going to expand on that later because that's another life event many of us have experienced, and it often leads to remorse later on. Maybe the demands of the job become too great, or the culture of the company asks more of us than we're willing to give at the moment. We pull the rip cord and give our notice without even considering what might happen if we stuck it out and worked through the discomfort. Later, when the company goes public, or when we realize that if we'd stayed we might be in the boss's chair by now, or we're fighting through the day-to-day monotony of yet another unsatisfying job (our third in as many years), we wish we'd done things differently.

The Swipe appears in nearly all areas of our lives. A near-universal instance comes when we tune out a loved one at an uncomfortable moment. Imagine that your child has come to you at a time of great vulnerability—maybe to ask you about an uncomfortable topic, maybe to share a bullying incident at school. But you're not ready to engage, or perhaps the topic disturbs you or you have other matters on your mind, so you Swipe. You disengage. You make an excuse about being tired or having work to do, and you turn away from a difficult conversation. Even if you may be physically present in the discussion, your mind is a thousand miles away. Yes, it's painful to think about, but it's even more painful to realize that you've just bypassed a pivotal moment that might never come again.

Swiping affects us all. We all disengage from things out of boredom, discomfort, panic, doubt, and fear. We all curate our own regrets in life by sprinting in the other direction rather than staying, letting things develop, and, when necessary, fighting the good fight. We Swipe in our work, relationships, creative lives, sports, educations, politics, even in our science, where unconscious bias can cause even the most rational scientists to overlook or even suppress data that doesn't fit their hypothesis. Swiping is everywhere.

Why We Wrote This Book

This book is the culmination of over two decades of research, surveying, data analytics, and interviews. We've lived this topic, both personally and through our research. Tim is a journalist with more than sixty books under his belt and has interviewed, written about, worked with, and written for professional athletes, seasoned executives, political figures, music and television artists, social influencers, and iconoclasts from many different walks of life. Tracy is a CEO, researcher, industrial-organizational psychologist, and university professor who has had the opportunity to study, learn from, coach, and work with thousands of leaders, students, and organizations for more than thirty years and in more than forty countries. Together we have seen individuals set the world on fire—and just as often, we've seen people disengage and flame out in a slow downward spiral, never having accomplished what they set out to do.

Many of the examples we use in this book are business-related. Why? While a great deal of our work revolves around the way individuals behave in organizations like businesses, that's not the primary reason. It's because a majority of us will spend one-third of our waking hours on the clock, doing what we do to earn a living. Employee engagement is a significant concern throughout the world, yet it's also something that organizations didn't think much about until perhaps the 1980s.

For more than two decades, we've been following the phenomenon of engagement in the workplace. In the past few years, employers have started sharing with us that despite all their efforts to "get their people to engage with the workplace and company culture"—the awards and training programs and team-building events and incentives—many are choosing not to engage.

In fact, estimates suggest that US companies invest more than $2 billion annually in employee engagement programs with little to show for their efforts.[5] Many justify this spending by claiming that the cost of disengagement far exceeds that $2 billion investment, with some estimates placing the cost of disengaged employees in the United States at in excess of $450 billion.[6] While that staggering figure may be hyperbole, the idea holds up to scrutiny.

Having worked with hundreds of companies and tens of thousands of managers, we realized we were hearing some common themes from company leaders. One CEO of a Fortune 100 company recently echoed what we have been hearing across the board. "We've spent the past five years focusing on improving our company culture," he said. "We've gotten rid of some bad managers. We have increased our compensation, built the best-in-industry benefits package, and instituted a company-wide flexible work policy. Yet our annual company survey results show very little change year over year. Sure, we're doing better, but our employees are still leaving the company. Ultimately, it's the employee's choice to engage. It's like they're choosing not to engage or think that they will be more engaged in the company down the street. We have great people! They just kind of 'check out.' I don't know what else we can do." His chief human resources officer echoed this sentiment.

When we took a closer look at what was happening, we realized an unexplored phenomenon was at play. Most employees were not consciously refusing to engage—we don't show up to work thinking, *I sure hope today sucks the life out of me*. Instead, they were reacting to uncomfortable circumstances by disengaging from what was in front of them. Perhaps the company was asking them to lead before they felt ready or expecting them to step into a role for which they had no experience. Perhaps the tasks of the day were not as appealing as other tasks they could have been doing. Maybe it's the allure of greener pastures, perks (the company down the street has Taco Tuesdays!), or a work-from-home promise. In any event, some quit altogether, while others stayed on the payroll but went through the motions, never fully committing to the company or its goals, sabotaging themselves and their employers. We all know someone who has mentally retired but still shows up every morning (in body, at least). Disengagement is a problem wherever we go. And that problem isn't just limited to business.

That was our "aha" moment. That's when we saw there was more involved in disengagement than simply being underwhelmed by an employer's attempts to win hearts and minds. There was something fundamental going on—some basic tenet of human behavior in mild distress, perhaps exacerbated by the ubiquity of technology that makes it incredibly easy to change our circumstances the moment they become unsatisfying. *Perhaps*, we thought, *this is a universal phenomenon*. Our past decade of research and a database of more than fifty million employee survey responses— the largest of its kind—confirmed the notion. Everyone Swipes. We all disengage, and it affects our success at work, our relationships with our loved ones, and our cherished goals and dreams. The Swipe determines a great deal about how our lives turn out, yet most of us are oblivious to its existence.

While we began looking at Swiping through the lens of business, the fundamental concepts and mechanisms of the Swipe affect us in every area of our lives. Most of us carry a weight of regret because of a business idea that never took off, a creative project left unfinished, or a romantic relationship that ended because somebody got cold feet. Swiping affects us all by scuttling our works of potential genius, preventing job-creating start-ups from getting off the ground, and sidetracking meant-to-be love. Companies miss chances to innovate and are crushed by nimble competitors. Cities waste millions on half-constructed roads and bridges to nowhere. As individuals, we go through life feeling cheated and ashamed, knowing we should try one more time to chase that big, hairy, audacious goal but finding ourselves paralyzed by our fear of losing our mojo and giving up *again*. We disengage and, in turn, miss out.

We wrote this book to change that. It doesn't have to be this way. There is hope! We can reengage. We can finish what we start more often and feel less of the helpless self-loathing that comes with quitting without accomplishing what is important to us. CEOs and bosses in all types of organizations can improve employee engagement after years of frustration and wasted investment, enjoying benefits like improved retention and a healthier culture. We're not talking about systems to set better goals or well-meaning tools to develop grit, though those can be helpful. Nothing will help us finish what we start until we can understand why so many of us cut and run as soon as things get dicey—*why* we Swipe.

That's what this book is about. We've tapped psychology, neurology, organizational observation, business, and old-fashioned horse sense to identify the predictable process that people go through when they Swipe, not to mention an alternate process they go through when they make the conscious choice to "resist and persist." As you can imagine, it's the latter path that tends to lead to completed projects, achieved goals, more worthwhile contribution, and greater satisfaction.

Through research, observation, and deduction, we've found the cognitive fork in the road where people tend to Swipe thoughtlessly out of panic or stress. We're going to share the secret to helping just about anybody reach that point, and when everything is on the line, make the right call: *not to Swipe.* By becoming aware of the psychological mechanism behind the Swipe, it's possible to stop quitting those cherished projects, potential dream jobs, or important relationships and actually see them through to the end. Imagine about how fulfilling it would be to find real joy in your work—not just that aspired-to perfect future job but the work you do *today.* Imagine what you could accomplish if you were fully engaged in what you did? Think of how much better—and happier—this world would be if we finished what we started. Think of how much happier and prouder you, your spouse, your child, your company, or your city would be.

Happiness, accomplishment, inner peace, success. It's all on the line here. As productivity expert David Allen said, "Much of the stress that people feel doesn't come from having too much to do. It comes from not finishing what they've started."

Time to change that. You ready?

CHAPTER 1

The Graveyard of Abandoned Dreams

> Swiping equals disengagement from the deep, meaningful experiences of life and work, which inevitably leads to unhappiness and disappointment.

By his twenties, Todd Crandell was on his way to becoming a cautionary tale. Once a promising hockey player with a future in the pros, he became addicted to drugs and alcohol, ruining not only his hockey career but every relationship in his life. Then, in 1993, he found his way to sobriety and turned his compulsive streak into a passion for endurance sports. Today Todd is an avowed vegan who has finished more than eighty-five Ironman and Ultraman endurance races, and he's the fittest fiftysomething you've ever set eyes on. He's also a licensed independent chemical dependency counselor and clinical supervisor who, in 2001, founded Racing for Recovery, an Ohio-based counseling community that works to prevent substance abuse and help people struggling with addiction discover a new lifestyle of fitness and health through sports.

That's quite a comeback story, and it's made Todd into something of an expert in endurance—more to the point, the act of not quitting. In endurance races like Ironman, competitors often say the winner is the one who can "outsuffer" everybody else. But what makes some competitors more able to gut through the agony of a marathon or a 112-mile bike leg? What keeps them from disengaging and pursuing something less taxing? To put it another way, what keeps them from Swiping? We asked Todd, who had competed in yet another Ironman the day before our conversation.

"Yesterday I had a great race," he said. "I swam well, I biked well, and then I got to the run, and suddenly I was sick and nauseous. So I'm out there, I'm walking a lot, and it's hot. I was thinking, *Why am I finishing this?* And there are two sides to the answer: First, it's wanting to succeed. I want to succeed and add another notch to my belt. I am grateful for the people who have helped me do what I do, and I owe it to them not to quit.

"Then there's another piece of it, which is that I don't want to fail. I'm starting to see that not only in myself but it's a common characteristic in people with addiction. We take that negative passion to self-destruct and turn it into self-improvement, and that means there's this constant fire: 'I won't be beaten this time. I'm not going to fail.' Used properly, it's a great asset.

"I think it's easier for people who haven't gone through the adversity of addiction—let's not sugarcoat it—to give up on things. When you make that life-or-death choice to get better, you can use all the heartbreaking, tumultuous situations you've put yourself and your loved ones through as fuel to succeed. It's an interesting psychology, or mindset, that really does become an asset."

Page-One Energy

What makes Todd Crandell and other ultraendurance athletes—not to mention those in other endeavors that demand perseverance in the face of physical or mental pain—tick isn't solely their athletic prowess. It's their will not to quit, their self-awareness, their commitment to remaining engaged in the moment, and their personal kit of psychological tricks and motivational tools—for example, mining the fear of failure—that keep them going when others fall away.

As the success of NaNoWriMo shows, in a complex world, simply sticking with something and finishing, regardless of the outcome, is often the real victory. We've stood at the finish line at the Ironman World Championships in Kailua-Kona, Hawaii, and watched amateur "age group" competitors labor agonizingly on the final mile along the famous Ali'i Drive, calling on their last reserves of energy to try and finish before the seventeen-hour cutoff. When they make it, even the last finishers get a hero's welcome. Why? Because they persisted. They remained engaged, even as their bodies were screaming at them to stop. They leaned into the pain and doubt and didn't Swipe.

Many competitors can't say that. Of course, some suffer injuries and are forced to drop out. That's not a Swipe. But others simply lack the will to keep going. Some never make it back to that hallowed course through the lava fields and regret it for the rest of their lives. Multiply that experience by millions in human activities as diverse as going back to college, getting in shape, composing a piece of music, or starting a company, and we see the same patterns play out again and again.

In the beginning, most people approach a new undertaking with a measure of naive enthusiasm—what we call *page-one energy*, a reference to the optimism of an author starting a new book. At this stage, things appear easy. You've got this. You're like a cyclist at the top of a hill, coasting down, propelled by gravity, the wind in your hair. This is fun! Whee!

Then you hit the bottom of the hill, and that giddy speed begins . . . to . . . slow. Gradually, it dawns on you that this will not be easy. This is *hard*. Now you have to pedal, and the pedaling grows harder and harder as you realize you now have a big hill to climb. Exultation turns to trepidation, then frustration, and even outrage. Easygoing fun has given way to ugly, sweaty *work*. Why didn't someone *tell* you it would be like this?

After a while you're not sure you can continue—or that you *want* to continue. Your page-one energy is gone, replaced by a dread of what comes next and whether or not you're up to it. Will you have the strength, resolve, skills, or whatever else you need to get this done? Were you an idiot to even try in the first place? As your self-doubt builds, the pressure to Swipe grows. Eventually, completely *disillusioned* by the experience, you slow to a stop. You tell yourself this challenge was stupid and didn't really matter anyway—the "whatever moment"—and you disengage, leaving the scene as quickly as you can rather than risk being shamed by others who faced the same hardship you did but found a way to keep going.

This was the experience of Australian triathlon legend Chris "Macca" McCormack. One of the greatest competitors in the history of the sport, McCormack struggled when he transitioned from cold-weather, short-course European triathlons to dare the Ironman in the heat and humidity of Hawaii. Year after year, starting in 2002, he came to the island ready to win but quit as heat and dehydration sapped his strength. His low point came in 2005. Overcome again by the searing heat, he dropped out of the race during the marathon leg and was sitting in an air-conditioned judge's car when he spotted an amateur competitor walking along the side of the road, carrying his bike and covered in lacerations, road rash, and blood.

The athlete had crashed during the cycling leg of the race, but determined to finish, he carried his crippled bike to the finish line—from where, presumably, he would attempt to run the marathon. McCormack said he never felt more ashamed than at that moment as he watched that man, competing for nothing but pride, keep going while he, the professional, had thrown in the towel.

The thought of competing in an Ironman might not get you out of bed in the morning—honestly, it doesn't appeal to us either. We have to admit, though, that we admire those who have the fortitude to complete the grueling race. Seeing that work project through to the end gives us a sense of satisfaction. Finishing your book, spending quality time with a loved one before he or she passes away, finishing a degree, nailing that hairy work project, or getting past a rough patch in a relationship is that Ironman you didn't finish. Swiping, however, leaves us humiliated and angry that, once again, we failed.

Swiping is Universal

The made-to-order world of smart devices might make Swiping more ubiquitous and even more tempting, but before you think we're going to label the Swipe as a millennial or Gen Z phenomenon, stop. We're not going to predictably gripe about peripatetic, tech-addicted youngsters who can't finish what they start. Younger people are no more likely to Swipe through life than boomers. Swiping is a *universal* phenomenon.

There's been little true scientific research into the phenomenon of quitting what we start, but there's been plenty into a Swipe-adjacent phenomenon: *procrastination*. According to work done by Joseph Ferrari, professor of psychology at DePaul University, 25 percent of people around the world are chronic procrastinators.[1] While one-fourth of the world fits this "chronic" label, nearly all of us fit somewhere on the don't-finish-what-we-start spectrum.

Research conducted at the University of Scranton found that 92 percent of people who set New Year's resolutions fail to achieve them[2]—which will come as no surprise to anyone who's sworn on December 31 to look like a runway model by beach season, only to reach the Fourth of July with only their wallet lighter after purchasing unused workout equipment.

But here's the big problem: according to research from Finder, 74.72 percent of all Americans planning to make New Year's resolutions for 2021 were confident they would achieve their resolutions.[3] That's a deep disconnect between aspiration and accomplishment. That's why the best evidence of the Swipe is literally the people around us. We all know dozens of family members, friends, peers, and colleagues who complain bitterly about the things they've meant to do for years but haven't done—big things, like going back to school, and seemingly small goals, like finishing household projects. You almost certainly have your own list of unfinished frustrations; we all do. That's why an undercurrent of discontent runs through life for so many of us. We know we're capable of more, but we just can't get there.

In 2014, when employee experience firm DecisionWise began researching "intent to stay" statistics (data on individuals who plan to remain with their current employers) they were surprised to find that, despite what many had claimed, fewer than 11 percent of employees had been actively circulating their résumés. Much of that lack of activity was likely related to a tough global job market. However, that number has increased dramatically. In 2022 CNBC reported that, according to studies conducted by consulting firm Willis Towers Watson, 44 percent of workers reported looking for a new job.[4] When given the opportunity to look around and compare our current situation to a hypothetical alternative, it seems we quickly become dissatisfied.

Swiping affects virtually every individual in every environment. Apart from the obvious examples we've already cited—work life, creative projects, weight loss—there are many others. College students who drop out after sophomore year because the work is too grueling are often Swiping, assuming that one day they'll circle back to finish their degree. Many never do. Nicotine is a highly addictive substance, making cigarette smoking a notoriously difficult habit to quit. Despite this, roughly 1.3 million Americans quit each year, but the individuals who fail are those who can't help but Swipe past the unpleasant physical and psychological sensations that come with nicotine withdrawal. They quickly pivot to the relief of a satisfying smoke, only to feel guilt and shame after they do.

The serial dater who ghosts potential partners as soon as casual dating becomes something more serious is a Swiper. So is the patient who fires their physician because said doctor gave them health advice they didn't want to follow, like losing weight or cutting saturated fats. Then there is the employee who is "just here for the paycheck until that dream job comes along."

Perhaps you know someone who is always working the next business angle—the friend who leaves one business venture for another under the pretense that the next big opportunity is just around the corner. We tend to idolize serial entrepreneurs—those who seem to have the Midas touch—as paragons of business moxie. But for every true entrepreneur, we find many more people who bounce from one business experiment to the next because they become bored or frustrated, or lose interest once the exhilaration of a startup fades into the day-to-day grind of running a company.

Declining to engage when things get difficult or complex doesn't just affect individuals either. We see it in organizations too. After years of researching engagement in the workplace and collecting millions of survey results from thousands of businesses, we know for certain that when people disengage—when they stop caring and recoil from the task or challenge in front of them—the results of their work suffer. Companies invest millions of dollars to encourage employee engagement because they know that when people disengage they don't just retreat from their own responsibilities. Their indifference and discontent affect and *infect* others. Quality slips, productivity drops, customer service declines, and turnover spikes. In a business setting, disengagement is a quiet, creeping disease that kills cultures and ruins organizations (heads up: we will discuss this more in chapter 4). But do you know what makes this even more dangerous? That bad job spills over into other areas of life as well; you take it home with you. More on this later.

Even giant corporations Swipe. Remember Blockbuster Video? If you're under thirty, you might not. That's because the retail video rental company, which dominated the video rental market back in the day when you and your friends had to drive to a store to rent movies on DVD and VHS, Swiped away from what might have been its salvation.

In 1999, two years after Blockbuster said, "Thanks, but no thanks," to buying Netflix for a paltry $50 million, the company teamed up with Enron—yes, *that* Enron—to create a robust video-on-demand platform. The result was a platform that worked and that customers liked. Blockbuster was poised to seize a substantial portion of the fledgling streaming market. But Blockbuster was so single-minded about its stores that it neglected the video-on-demand service. In 2001 they completely abandoned it, and by 2010 the company was bankrupt. Meanwhile, despite some setbacks in 2022, Netflix has become the dominant brand in streaming entertainment.

Governments Swipe too. The People's Republic of China got into the act with the medieval-themed Wonderland, which it insisted would become the largest, grandest amusement park in Asia. When the Chinese government got into an endless series of disputes with local officials and farmers, however, the half-finished project was abandoned in 1998. An attempt to restart development in 2008 also flopped, and the park was finally demolished in 2013. In its place now stands an outlet mall.

NERD ALERT!

For software developers, Swiping is a work-around for choice paralysis, the inability to make a decision because you're overwhelmed by too many options. A swipe-centric interface for, say, e-commerce, lets users view one option at a time so they're less likely to become exhausted and disengage altogether from the product choices in front of them.

A Formula for Unhappiness

That familiar process not only leads inexorably to misery but it impedes our growth. Angela Duckworth, author of the bestselling book *Grit: The Power of Passion and Perseverance*, writes that the key to reaching goals is about holding steadfast to them even after you fall down or make mistakes, or when progress toward the goal is agonizingly slow. Grit is the quality that makes that possible. But we develop grit through trial and error, through the water torture of failure, embarrassment, and heartache. Recovering from setbacks—and discovering they don't end us—makes us strong.

But what about those times we don't get off the mat after being knocked down—or worse, don't even get into the ring? When we Swipe, we deny ourselves the opportunity to rise to the occasion and prove we have what it takes to succeed. Human beings are at our best when we're striving, working to overcome obstacles. When our backs are against the wall, that's when we find courage and creativity we didn't know we had. But without that tension and resolution, it's easy to become apathetic and defeatist. Over time, this leads to regret, dissatisfaction, and unhappiness.

Then, after we've pulled the rip cord and bailed out of the plane, what do we do? We beat ourselves up. Quitting something shames us. We feel like we're missing some magical "get-it-done" gene. Swipe often enough, and you begin to believe you don't have what it takes, that you're not worthy. Instead of mastering what you care about, you just master the Swipe.

Psychology even has a term to describe how we feel when we leave things undone: the Zeigarnik effect.[5] If we are engaged in a task that's interesting but not impossibly difficult, we feel distress and frustration when we don't complete it, coupled with a compulsion to go back and get to the finish line. The Zeigarnik effect might also explain why we regret the things we *didn't* do—so-called "regrettable omissions"—more than the things we did.[6]

Pre-Swipe Warning Signs

Let's review. We have identified a clear, predictable psychological and emotional process that people go through when they Swipe, and an equally clear path showing what happens when we decline to Swipe and engage with our discomfort. We'll get to that process later, but right now it's important to understand the conditions that lead us to Swipe.

Swiping is typically preceded by a state of benign self-delusion, usually about how difficult the task before you will be. In fact, not apprehending how hard it will be to reach your goal is a powerful predictor of a future Swipe. For example, a child might believe learning to play the piano will be all about playing flawless chords and sweeping arpeggios in a matter of days, not endlessly playing scales, which is the bane of every piano novice's existence. Or a man might believe that because he's watched lots of *This Old House* episodes and owns a hammer drill he's ready to build a wooden deck off the back of his house, only to find he has no idea what he's doing. The presumption that the glide path to success will be smooth and easy creates false expectations of what lies ahead, and this often causes the person to venture into a complex task with lots of page-one energy and little else.

That page-one energy is the base for our motivation. But motivation is a fickle partner, despite the fact that we think the same energy we experience on page 1 will be with us through page 250. We rely on motivation, however, to carry us through—"future motivation," that is. As we begin, we mistakenly believe the "future me" will have the same motivation as the "in-the-moment me." This is why we sign up for gym memberships, buy that hammer drill, register for free online classes, and sign up for diet plans. The current me wants it and is energized by the promises made by in-the-moment me's page-one energy. The future me? Not so much. Today's me's bursts of motivation make promises the future me doesn't find as energizing.

When a reversal inevitably comes—running out of gas at page sixty of that novel, discovering that a job promotion requires more than three months of employment, discovering that earning a black belt in karate takes years, finding out you don't know a ledger board from a rim joist—it triggers a *disillusionment event* similar to the action-provoking *inciting event* in a movie screenplay. Reality shatters your false perceptions that achieving your goal would be relatively effortless, leaving you bitterly disillusioned and over- whelmed. When people reach that disillusioning event, and they have no tools or mental processes to help them stay on course and not lose faith in themselves, they almost always Swipe.

Having accurate, specific foreknowledge of how challenging a goal will be to reach reduces the odds of Swiping. When you know that building a deck or training for a 10K will take time, require rigorous preparation, and come with several setbacks, you won't be as thrown by reversals or be as apt to become fatally discouraged, because you already knew this journey would come with bumps. You give yourself a break, jump back in, and keep pushing.

HOW NOT TO SWIPE

Before you take your first step toward a goal or into unfa- miliar territory, give yourself some "Swipe insurance" by reciting and remembering this Harry Belafonte–inspired acronym: DAYO, which stands for Don't Assume You're the Outlier. When you're confronting something you haven't done before, avoid the mistake so many others have made and don't kid yourself that the lessons learned by those who came before you—it's grueling, study hard, give yourself enough time, etc.—don't apply to you. In reality, they almost always do. Don't assume you're smarter, braver, more gifted, or tougher than anyone else. You will be better prepared for what's to come and will increase your chances of reaching the finish line.

Tapping Out—How Swiping Changes Us

Each of us will disengage at times. As we detail later in this book, it's part of our psychological and physical programming. There will always be moments where we disengage, where we're simply not dedicating our hearts, spirits, minds, or hands to what is in front of us. But that doesn't always result in a Swipe.

Every time we Swipe away from difficulty, we veer away from a different and potentially promising future. When you hit that critical crossroads, where you can either Swipe or engage with something hard, it's generally not a time for deep thought and consideration. Swiping is a reflexive action, not a mental or emotional process. Nevertheless, when you Swipe, you're choosing one of the paths that leads away from that crossroads, like someone in a Robert Frost poem. Swiping is taking one road at a fork and not looking back. When you do that, you will miss out on everything that might be found down the other road, including the potential to grow or find happiness.

Former financial consultant and ecclesiastical leader Stanley G. Ellis recounts his experiences in working with multimillionaires in Texas who were successful entrepreneurs. Most had built successful businesses from the ground up, facing numerous trials and hard work along the way. According to Ellis, one of the saddest things to hear was that some of them wanted to make life easier for their children by ensuring their children didn't suffer as they had. As caring as this parental wish might have been, Ellis lamented, "In other words, they would deprive their children of the very thing that had made them successful." Whether it's for ourselves or for those we love, that tough love and the learning it brings is what makes us who we are. Yet most of us would prefer to take the easier fork, and many of us—and our children—learn to reactively Swipe to the path of least resistance.[7]

But there are instances in which this choice is conscious. When it is, deliberate thought precedes action. That's not a Swipe. That's what we call *tapping out*. Sometimes abandoning a project or ending a relationship is a perfectly rational, even empowering decision. It's not always a bad idea to move on from something that isn't working. The difference lies in the psychological mechanism. When you Swipe, you're not making a deliberate decision to disengage or quit. You're recoiling out of alarm, like someone ducking away from an explosion. When you tap out, you're weighing the evidence and making a call that says, "This is not right for me, and I'm electing to step away." While Swiping is often fraught with regret and disappointment, tapping out can be courageous and positive.

Consider US gymnast Simone Biles at the 2021 Summer Olympics. When she bowed out of the women's all-around competition because she had developed the "twisties"—a gymnastics term for becoming spatially disoriented in midair during potentially dangerous leaps or vaults—there was no panic involved. There was no, "Ah, I just don't wanna do it, so I'm going to try something new for a change."

Instead, she made a brave, proactive decision to look after her own physical and mental health, even though doing so likely cost her a gold medal. She was quite rightfully praised for her decision.

Another example is former army intelligence officer and Missouri secretary of state Jason Kander. A young, rising Democratic star, after losing the 2016 race for the US Senate, Kander announced his candidacy for mayor of Kansas City, Missouri. Then, in October 2018, he announced he was quitting politics for the foreseeable future, revealing his battles with posttraumatic stress disorder, depression, and suicidal thoughts. As with Biles, this was not a Swipe, but a measured, intentional choice in Kander's best interest. He chose to put his mental health and his family—not to mention his advocacy group Let America Vote, a nonprofit that fights against voter suppression efforts—before a perceived obligation to remain a candidate.

It's true that Swiping and tapping out can lead us to the same destination. After all, in either case, we're not finishing what we set out to do. The difference, however, lies in who we are when we get off that side path and back to the main road. Swiping can leave a bitter taste of shame and surrender in its wake. Tapping out, on the other hand, is knowingly walking away from something that's poorly suited to our skills or aspirations while choosing to engage in something more beneficial. Quitting a job with terrible hours, leaving an abusive partner, dropping out of college to pursue a lifelong dream via another means, these aren't Swipes. These are affirmative acts of self-love and self-preservation that give us room to heal and become more completely who we are.

The act of Swiping affects us in a variety of negative ways:

- **Bypassing**—In dodging uncomfortable situations and feelings, we also dodge opportunities to discover new abilities and dimensions of ourselves that might never come again. People who do this often become fearful that they will never complete tasks or reach goals because failure becomes their new normal.

- **Stasis**—If the Swipe becomes habitual, we don't progress and grow. We don't take the opportunity to stretch and learn, which leads to stagnation. We remain stuck in a state of nonchallenge that feels safe but is actually detrimental.
- **Fatalism**—Like the would-be author who, after multiple unsuccessful attempts to finish a novel, berates herself, "See? I'll never be a real writer," repeated Swipes can eventually lead us to conclude that we can't finish things and that nothing in our lives will ever change.

But the most dangerous effect of the Swipe is that it's corrosive to our *self-efficacy*, the belief that we have what it takes to meet challenges and achieve success in situations that matter to us. Self-efficacy and self-esteem are closely linked, and when someone continually fails to finish what they start and misses cherished goals, their belief in their ability to achieve what's important—their belief in their fortitude, strength, and will—erodes until it crumbles like an old stone seawall.

One reason for that is that disengagement doesn't equal dissolution. When you Swipe, what you disengage with typically doesn't go away. It's still out there, having an impact on your life. Call off the wedding the day before the ceremony because of cold feet, and you might breathe a temporary sigh of relief, but you still have a lot of people who want you dead. When you Swipe, you lay traps for yourself that you can't even see, but that often come back to haunt you in the future.

Swiping is a short-term action, but it can have consequences that last for years. But the situation isn't hopeless. As we'll demonstrate, it is possible to "take back" a Swipe if we act quickly. We can also learn to resist the temptation to Swipe and engage with what we've been avoiding, gaining the opportunity to grow and discover our strengths. So maybe it's time we understood how and why the Swipe happens. Let's dig deeper into the mechanics of what's happening when we Swipe and how we can take control of this universal human experience.

CHAPTER 2

Swipeland

> It's critical to understand the expectations surrounding the Swipe and what's waiting for us in the aftermath. There is regret, of course, but there are a host of other mental destinations we visit when we give up on something and enter an imaginary world of our own design.

Amelia Alvin is a practicing psychiatrist in Miami, Florida. You would think that level of accomplishment—getting into and surviving medical school, becoming a physician, building a successful psychiatric practice—would be enough for anyone. But we're complicated creatures who tend to covet what we don't have. We believe, without evidence, that the grass will be greener on *that* side of the fence. Or perhaps we're just ambitious and restless. In any case, Amelia (like her namesake, Ms. Earhart) dreamed of becoming a pilot.

"Being a pilot was my dream while growing up," she wrote in response to our questions. "After graduating, I got myself enrolled at a private flying club. That was a fantasy come true. I had my first flight of one-and-a-half hours with a senior instructor. The first time I held the controls, the feel of being empowered was priceless. It seemed like I got wings. One year down the line, I gave up on the only thing that made me feel alive. But there were reasons why I could not finish what I started.

"First, loss of motivation. Being a short-tempered human, I always demand immediate results. If I don't see any improvement shortly, I get cold feet. Second, time frame. Sometimes people don't meet their target because it gets hard for them to manage time and spare moments for a newly added agenda in an already-hectic schedule. I was supposed to fly five hours weekly to get my license. Time is a key constraint to finish the things we start.

"Finally, no support. Little support and few resources lead to leaving a task in the lurch. Despite everything, I still plan to get committed to my goals all over again sometime in life."

That's a familiar story. But if a trained mental health professional can't push past the natural obstacles to finishing what we start, do the rest of us have any hope? We do. Sometimes the failure to call something "finished" has nothing to do with not reaching a goal but with aspiring to continue and grow without ever really being "done."

Samantha Harding, a businesswoman and fashion designer, described her journey to get her brand, Sahar Swimwear, off the ground: "I started Sahar eight years ago, and I haven't finished it," she wrote. "It's my baby, which I started in college. As it grows, I see that it will never have a finish date. It's one of those things that, as I grow, will follow my journey with me and grow too. The mission and vision have evolved as I evolve. My vision is to be the largest resort-wear brand on earth, so this will be a never-ending mission in my life. I have been thrown off track with a bad relationship, a car accident, family, but sometimes, when your mission and passion are stronger than anything, you still continue."

So why doesn't this add up? Dr. Alvin had a passion for flying, but she wasn't able to get her license. Samantha has been able to push past multiple obstacles and keep building her company. What's the X factor that separates the people who push past busy schedules, disruptive life events, natural fears and doubts, or a lack of resources to continue to engage and achieve their goals from the ones who don't? As with any discussion related to human psychology and behavior, there's more than one answer. But part of the answer lies in understanding what happens after we Swipe—the psychological games we play to blunt our remorse, the justifications we lay out to avoid passing cruel judgment on ourselves, and so on.

The Science of Failure

In general, the act of Swiping past an uncomfortable reality is also the act of arresting our own natural process of growth and self-discovery. We learn best from facing up to our mistakes and correcting them, not by running from them. Because it's reflexive, impulsive, and a response to anxiety, Swiping is dysfunction masquerading as a solution. In Swiping, we deny ourselves the opportunity to fail authentically—to see a task or activity through to fruition and then confront what we did well and what we did poorly, like a student looking at the questions he or she got wrong on an exam.

We swap out that "productive failure," which also comes with some measure of accomplishment, for the true failure of refusing to finish at all. We focus on the superficial, and as a result we never learn about ourselves. We deny ourselves the opportunity to go in different directions, find joy in the unexpected, and become who we were meant to be.

The "fail forward fast" doctrine extolled everywhere from *Forbes* articles to TED talks reflects the important role that seeing things through to the end, complete with errors and stumbles, plays in learning and growth. People in business at all levels are encouraged to take risks, think big, and pursue so-called "moon shots." With bold initiatives come expected failures, but this way of thinking treats failures as stepping-stones to discovery and eventual triumph. When a project or product falls flat, its architects do a forensic analysis of what went wrong, identify things that need correction, and try, try again. That iterative process is free of blame or shame. In fact, the only shame is in not proposing ideas that are audacious enough, or in not seeing the work through to the bitter end.

Viewed through the lens of the Swipe, we might be justified in redefining the meaning of the word *failure*. To this point, popular culture has largely defined *failure* as a planned-for outcome not working out according to the plan—a product prototype flopping in testing, or a political candidate losing on election day. But in those defeats lie the embers of future victory. In striving and working to completion, we gain self-knowledge, develop new skills, build teams and collaborative coalitions, and lay bare our own weaknesses, which we can then address.

Genuine failure, then, may be the purview of Rosie Ruiz and others who didn't have what it took and quit—or worse, cheated. Ruiz was the infamous Cuban runner declared the winner of the 1980 Boston Marathon, only to have the title stripped from her eight days later, when it was discovered she had entered the race-course halfway through. There's nobility and wisdom in attempting something that's outrageous, even doomed. But when, like Ruiz, we simply give up, or worse, act dishonestly in order to finish for the sake of finishing, we don't grow. That's the true failure.

The disgrace isn't in falling on our faces. It's never getting out of our chairs.

Empirical research shows that productive failure is even a prerequisite for success. Dashun Wang, professor of management and organizations at Northwestern University's Kellogg School of Management, analyzed 776,721 grant applications submitted to the National Institutes of Health between 1985 and 2015. His team's goal was to create a mathematical model that would reliably predict whether a venture would succeed or fail, based in part on an analysis of forty-six years of venture capital investments.

Wang and his colleagues found that all successful ventures occurred after the people involved tried and failed multiple times to achieve their goals. The difference maker was not persistence, as one might think, but the ability to learn from past failures.[1] A failure of plans carried out to fruition but derailed by human error, technical failure, accident, or unforeseeable circumstance tends to be a marvelous teacher, revealing the flaws in our strategies and our execution.

When we Swipe, we forfeit that learning experience. Stung by our lack of follow-through and sprinting away from the prospect of confronting it face-to-face, we learn nothing, ensuring that we're nearly certain to repeat the same mistakes.

THE GIRL ON THE TRAIN

For years we've been obsessed with the 2014 National Geographic photo contest winner, a photo titled "A Node in the Dark." The winning image, captured by Brian Yen, shows people riding a crowded train attraction at Hong Kong's Ocean Park amusement park. Riders are shoulder to shoulder in the blue-and-amber scene, but one spotlit young woman stands out: engrossed by her smartphone, completely isolated from the throng surrounding her. A write-up in the *Atlantic* gushes over the woman in the image as "a node flickering on the social web, roaming the Earth, free as a butterfly,"[2] but we see something more sinister. We see an individual, surrounded by others also engrossed in what's on their microscreens, for whom disengagement from reality has become habitual, enabled by the allure of technology. It's her way of existing in the world, of customizing her experience so she doesn't have to engage with anything not personally curated and approved. That withdrawing from the real into the digital represents the danger of the Swipe: that Swiping becomes our default way of being in the world, and we lose the ability to recognize and appreciate the spontaneous and imperfect as sources of growth and joy in our lives.

A Taxonomy of Swipes

The trajectory of the Swipe as a malfunction of the will to strive looks the same regardless of the circumstances. The Swipe of a frustrated novelist plays out in a similar way to that of a marriage-spooked boyfriend running for the hills. But like Tolstoy's famous opening line in *Anna Karenina* about unhappy families, all Swipes are different in their own way. That is to say, the internal *justifications* for Swiping differ greatly from individual to individual.

Understanding the circumstances under which we feel justified in Swiping, and our rationales for doing so, can help us identify the patterns in our own behavior and make it more likely that we will refuse to Swipe, or at least hesitate before doing so.

We humbly present, for your edification, a field guide to the varied species of Swipes most commonly found in the wilderness of human behavior, an encomium of benign self-delusions running headfirst into the plate glass of reality, a graveyard of orphaned dreams—a taxonomy of Swipes.

Goodness, that was a bit melodramatic, wasn't it? Noted. Onward.

- **The Intimidation Swipe**—The most common type of Swipe. It occurs when we are well past the starting line of a new project or goal, and we come face-to-face with just how difficult and challenging it will be to achieve the goal we've set for ourselves. This Swipe is a product of the lack of investigation and preparation common to Swipers. Picture an inexperienced cyclist who dreams of competing in the Tour de France and takes to the hills and mountain roads near his home, only to come face-to-face with the fact that experienced cyclists enjoy a level of fitness he can barely comprehend. Daunted by the prospect of gaining that same level of fitness, he says, "Never mind."
- **The Disillusionment Swipe**—This Swipe is a cousin to the first, but instead of being intimidated by what lies ahead, the individual gets well into the pursuit of a goal and then finds it's just not as much *fun* as they thought it would be. We see this often with novice writers. From the outside, the prospect of conjuring fantastic characters and splendid alternate worlds a la J. K. Rowling or J. R. R. Tolkien—what is it with

fantasy authors going by their initials, anyway?—seems like playtime, like riding a roller coaster at a theme park with perfect weather and no lines. They sit down at their computers with the germ of an idea and little else, write thirty-five pages at a fever pitch, and then, gradually, the roller coaster slows to a stop. The ideas have dried up. The giddy page-one energy is gone. What remains is the heavy lift of invention, of planning and plotlines and character studies. This is *work*! Without an accountability structure, like NaNoWriMo, to keep them going, most close the laptop, promise to get back to their book at a later date, and simply never do.

- **The Ennui Swipe**—The mental process here is similar to that of the Disillusionment Swipe, but the provocation is different. The individual gets past the early-stage optimism of a new goal, but now that they're neck-deep in the activity, it's pretty dull. Having gotten past the entrancing exterior, what's inside the box just isn't all that interesting. This Swipe also plays out frequently in the workplace, particularly with younger, less experienced employees. They enter the job market filled with idealism and lofty ambitions, start a new job, and quickly see that building a dream career takes years, even decades. Drudgery leads to torpor leads to resignation.

- **The Greener Grass Swipe**—This person swipes after looking around constantly for a better situation than the one they're in and finally thinks they see it. Blissfully unaware that they're playing out a pattern that's repeated itself several times before, they jump ship. This scenario is also quite common in business, where employees impulsively dash for the exit before they've even given a job or a new position a chance, convincing themselves irrationally that the *next* gig will be a perfect fit—and if not, the one after *that*. We also see this Swipe in romantic relationships. A few months into the relationship, the haze of lust has cleared, and one partner finally sees the other as a flawed human being. Or perhaps the pair are a few years into a marriage, and the famed "itch" has set in. One partner is bored with the relationship and develops a wandering eye. In either case, the restless lover eventually decides that being with that attractive person over there *must* be better than staying the course. Of course, as we know, the doctrine of "wherever you go, there you are" comes into play, and the relationship on the other side of the fence doesn't work out either, but that's a subject for a different book.

- **The Inspector Javert Swipe**—Now we come to the person who fears finishing the task or achieving the goal. We've named this Swipe after Inspector Javert from Victor Hugo's *Les Misérables*, who pursued the wrongly accused Jean Valjean until the pursuit came to define his life. People who Swipe in this situation typically fall into two camps. In one, like Javert, the pursuit itself has come to define them. They're the people whose friends are always asking them, "How's that screenplay you've been working on going?" If they ever finished the work, they don't know what they would do with their time or what they would talk about with friends. The second camp is the people who fear the judgment of others. They're afraid that if they finish their painting and exhibit it critics will savage them. If they say they've reached their fitness goal, unimpressed colleagues might say, "Oh, well, you look fine." It's safer to fall short than to lose one's identity or be judged as wanting.

- **The Impostor Syndrome Swipe**—This individual Swipes when the pursuit of a goal or the rigor of a job triggers insecurities that make them feel like a fraud. Impostor syndrome is not a recognized psychological disorder, but it's acknowledged by mental health professionals and personal performance coaches as a pattern of behavior in which people doubt their accomplishments and fear being exposed as incapable, incompetent, or unworthy.[3] Ironically, many individuals who fall victim to this Swipe are exceptionally accomplished, talented, and/or well educated. Yet when they get to depth, either in a professional position or as part of a personal pursuit, they become terrified that everyone will see they don't have what it takes. Better to quit than to suffer that humiliation.
- **The Ego Swipe**—This is the "I deserve better" Swipe that individuals engage in when they feel something is beneath them, is unfair in relation to what they perceive others have, or simply isn't worth their effort. We see this often in the workplace, where employees who feel slighted or underestimated will hit eject rather than lower themselves to do work that's beneath them, or be subordinate to someone else. For example, a newly promoted manager might quit in a fit of pique when asked to answer phones or pack boxes during a busy time.
- **The Trapped Animal Swipe**—This is the purest panic Swipe of all, most often seen in situations that require a long-term commitment—impending marriages; choices related to a demanding career path, such as medical school or law school; buying a home; or something similar. The individual feels terror at the idea of the commitment for one of many

reasons—from self-doubt to coercion—melts down, and runs, often leaving behind carnage and irretrievably lost opportunity.

Are you a Greener Grass Swiper? An Ego Swiper? A Disillusionment Swiper? Why on earth does it matter? It matters because when we recognize the motivating forces behind even our least-examined, most reactive behaviors, we gain some power to curb them—or at least to question them.

After You Swipe, Where Do You Expect to Go Next?

If our unconscious justifications for Swiping are the chocolate in the disengagement Reese's, our expectations of what will happen *after* we Swipe are the peanut butter. We've alluded to the ways that misaligned or pie-in-the-sky expectations can impact the likelihood of Swiping, but we haven't really dug into how powerful those expectations really are.

Psychologists and physicians have. They've been taking a long look at the *placebo effect*, in which patients given sham medication or treatment show improvement in a health condition—often a greater improvement than test subjects who receive the authentic medication or treatment. Today researchers note a similar effect in many other areas of human activity.

Imaging studies show that expectations of a wine's quality based on its price change how the brain's pleasure centers respond to a sip. Powerlifters have been shown to beat their personal bests when they believe they've taken a performance-boosting supplement, whether or not they really have. Experiments have even shown that people who hold powerful, superheroesque poses show hormonal changes similar to those who hold positions of genuine power and authority. In a nutshell, expectations do more than anticipate reality—they shape it.

Similarly, our expectations can powerfully influence our Swiping experience. True, when we Swipe, we don't do so with our expectations foremost in mind. The Swipe is not reflective but *reflexive*. When we pull that internal rip cord, we're just bailing out of the plane. We're not worrying very much about where we're going to land.

But once the brief exultation of not being stuck in that job, project, or relationship ebbs, we naturally develop expectations about what's next. One of the functions of our neocortex, the youngest and most advanced part of our brains, is to anticipate and predict the future. The problem is, in the same way that our pre-Swipe expectations— what we're capable of, how difficult our goal will be to achieve—tend to be warped, so too do our post-Swipe expectations.

Post-Swipe expectations are less about what we're capable of and more about convincing ourselves that our post-Swipe state will increase our happiness. Surely we didn't walk away from a two-year relationship for nothing, or quit a good-paying job without being certain that something better is on the horizon, right?

Right?

Imagine if, rather than protecting our egos and self-esteem by assuming our new post-Swipe situation will be better, we stopped for a second and asked, "What's most likely to happen after I pass the point of no return?" Note that we're not asking if the new circumstances will be better or worse, just what's probable. Is leaving one job likely to lead to bliss at the next? Really? Injecting some healthy skepticism into our expectations can blunt their placebo painkilling effect and remind us that the grass is, in fact, not always greener on the other side of the fence.

Skepticism is important, because the nonreflective nature of Swiping means we're always concocting a *post hoc* narrative. Rather than analyzing the evidence beforehand, the Swipe leaves us searching for justification for our actions after the fact. Desperate to avoid confronting the consequences of Swiping, we replace whatever we Swiped away from with something new that allows us to harbor the *illusion* that we've made a choice that will turn out better.

There are predictable destinations where we expect to land after Swiping, destinations that can be best explained using a jaunty world-travel metaphor.

What We Swipe To—Tropical Beach Edition

Swipe destination one is all about escape. We cut and run from a rough task still battered and sore, and we want to believe whatever is on the other side of the Swipe will be easier. And perhaps it will be, purely from the standpoint of effort. After all, we're no longer pounding the pavement training for a 10K or getting bleary-eyed studying for a degree that seemed like a good alternative to the job market. Why wouldn't that be easier?

You already know the answer to that question: Guilt. Regret. Remorse. The "Why can't I ever finish anything?" self-accusation. The temporary ease of Swiping comes at a high cost: accrued damage to our self-esteem.

What We Swipe To—Hometown Edition

Swipe destination two is a quest for the familiar and comfortable, and what's more familiar than going back to our hometowns? This might seem like solace to a wounded ego after making a panicked run for the exits, but it's really a flight from adult responsibility and consequences—a desperate retreat into childhood, where there are no difficult decisions or regrets on the horizon.

But as Thomas Wolfe wrote, you can't go home again. More accurately, you can try, but it's impossible to recapture the past. When we try to soothe our remorse by immersing ourselves in the familiar and unthreatening, we deny ourselves the chance to rise above the circumstances and grow. Nobody wants to be a child forever.

What We Swipe To—Day Spa Edition

We like our metaphors big, so destination three is everyone's default for hitting the reset button, the spa. Post-Swipe, we're hoping to forget all about the recent struggle and rest. Hitting reset, rebooting—call it what you will, but the ego slap that comes with walking away from a pursuit we care about is so harsh that we want to rewrite history—to pretend it wasn't *really* that important.

Of course it was. Denial is a classic symptom of regret. It's too painful to face our failures, so we create a fiction in which they never occurred. There are no mirrors to be found in this day spa. Unfortunately, that robs us of the chance to take a long look at ourselves and find a way to be successful next time—because, for better or worse, there will be a next time.

What happens when someone Swipes with no awareness of the destinations or the taxonomy? The same thing that's happened to a woman who's a close friend of ours. She's brilliant but mercurial and impulsive, forever jumping into jobs and career paths with little forethought and then heading for the hills the moment the gig becomes unpleasant or dull. As a result, this gifted designer has held more than twenty full-time jobs since her early thirties, most for less than one year. Somehow, because she's incredibly gifted and quite charismatic, new employers keep taking a chance on her.

One consequence of this game of musical careers is that this woman, now in her midfifties, has amassed no personal wealth or financial stability, having rarely stayed in one place long enough to vest in a retirement program. She owns no home and has no savings. Yet to this day she makes one Greener Grass Swipe after another in search of the perfect job, when in fact the perfect job doesn't exist.

HOW NOT TO SWIPE

It's asking a lot of anyone to expect flawless self-awareness, especially in the face of the panic that precedes the Swipe. So how can we avoid falling into these cognitive fallacies and making the Swipe that much worse? One possible preventive measure is to create consequences for Swiping that exist independently of anything you might do. For example, tell all your friends and colleagues about your Pacific Crest Trail hike so there's the threat of substantial social shame if you quit. One commercial example of this is the weight-loss program HealthyWage. Simply, when you sign up for the program, you place a monthly bet on hitting your weight goal. If you fail, you forfeit your bets. The tactic seems to work: a study published in the *Journal of the American Medical Association* found that having a financial incentive makes people five times more likely to reach their weight-loss goals than people who have no money at stake.[4] In other words, if you want to avoid Swiping, ensure that you will suffer pain if you do.

The Lies We Tell Ourselves

In his book, *The Lies We Tell Ourselves: How to Face the Truth, Accept Yourself, and Create a Better Life*, psychotherapist Jon Frederickson writes, "We often avoid the truths of our lives by waiting for fantasies to become true rather than face what is true."[5] Magical thinking is a hallmark of the Swipe. How else can we describe a withdrawal from a goal and the eventual return to the pursuit of that goal under the same circumstances as the last time, with just as much cockeyed optimism as before?

What makes repeated Swipes possible and even tolerable for some people are the carefully guarded lies we consume to armor ourselves from the pangs of regret. These are the self-deceptions that are agonizingly transparent when we see them in others, but stubbornly persistent when we engage in them ourselves.

The first great lie is, "I'll get back to it." It implies that even if someone abandons a goal in midstream, no worries, because they'll return to the chase someday, and then everything will be different. This is often done with the best of intentions. Of course, perhaps more often than not, someday never comes, and the challenge and opportunity are swept away by the demands of life.

The second big lie is, "Next time, things will be different." This the most delusional of the lies. What we often don't realize is that we are really implying, "*I* will be different." Even if there is a next time to attempt the novel, take on a challenging work project, or complete the long-distance bike ride, nothing is likely to change without deliberate changes in the individual's thinking, preparation, expectations, and understanding of the Swipe. Behavior rarely changes significantly without self-awareness and self-candor, not to mention consequences. With so many mechanisms available to allow us to dodge all the above, it's no wonder that often things are not at all different the second time around.

The third lie is, "It's not the right time." This is a sibling of the excuse many of us toss out when we're hesitating to start something big: "I'll know when I'm ready." In both cases, we excuse our failure to act by inventing a rationale that blames our lack of action on bad timing. With the Swipe, we didn't quit because we were scared or unprepared or naive; we quit because the stars simply hadn't aligned. In a few months or years, when we're more experienced, have more time, or when there's some sort of harmonic convergence, we're sure to succeed.

The next lie is, "It's not me, it's you." While most of our big lies are related to our own internal monologue, this one focuses on external causes. Think back to what we heard from our CEO: "Ultimately, it's the employee's choice to engage. It's like they're choosing not to engage or think that they will be more engaged in the company down the street. We have great people! They just kind of 'check out.' I don't know what else we can do."

It's convenient to blame disengagement on the external environment. In the workplace, for example, rather than accepting the fact that our lack of engagement is the result of a Swipe, we criticize the organization. Research, however, doesn't support that conclusion. In our studies on employee engagement, we found that the average organization carries just 12 to 18 percent of the responsibility when it comes to its employees' engagement in their work. In other words, most of an employee's choice to engage isn't the result of what the organization does. But it's usually easier to blame someone else—the company, the ex-boyfriend, the professor, or city council—for our disengagement. Why? Because we're absolved of responsibility, and more importantly, guilt.

This is a dodge. Nothing forces us to disengage; we choose to disengage. In the words of the acclaimed philosopher (and old-timey comic strip character) Pogo, "We have met the enemy and he is us."

The final big lie is related to impostor syndrome: "I was never going to be able to do it anyway." This lie is related to another, which psychologists often refer to as the sour-grape effect. Inspired by Aesop's fables, this downplaying of the value of unattainable goals has us telling ourselves, "It wasn't that important anyway." In the fable, a fox finds his way to a vineyard, where he stretches for a bunch of grapes but is unable to reach them. After several attempts, the fox gives up, stating, "They were probably sour anyway."

When we cast doubt on our ability to close the deal or reach the finish line, we're creating a "pre-excuse" for failure, a rationale that our goal wasn't desirable in the first place. If we weren't ever capable of succeeding, or if that pot at the end of the rainbow was empty, we lose nothing in giving up, right?

But the lies we tell ourselves are more than safeguards against regret. They can also become part of our inner narrative, trotted out again and again like worn-out jokes at a cocktail party and used to give us a never-ending free pass for failure. Rather than hold ourselves accountable and accept the emotional cost, we make it easy to skip out on the check. Nothing changes.

That is the tragedy of the Swipe. Nothing changes. We desperately want to grow, achieve goals, and be worthy in the face of challenges. But we can't, because we don't give ourselves the chance. The final products of Swiping are ennui, discouragement, disillusionment, fatalism, and regret. But so what? Everybody's unhappy about something, right? Perhaps, but there's a lot more to the consequences of Swiping.

CHAPTER 3

The Human Cost of the Swipe

> Constantly flitting from situation to situation to avoid dis-
> comfort robs us of the potential for self-discovery, catharsis,
> and joy, and it denies us the privilege of having our precon-
> ceptions and biases challenged, giving us little chance to
> evolve and learn empathy.

Click was a 2006 science-fiction comedy film directed by Frank Coraci and produced by and starring Adam Sandler. Widely panned by critics, it was a forgettable movie—except that it carries a metaphor that's especially relevant to the Swipe.

In *Click*, Sandler plays Michael, an overworked architect who neglects his family. Then, for reasons that remain unclear, he's given a magical remote control by a stranger. But instead of controlling his television, this remote lets him control the progression of time around him. He can reverse to replay certain moments, stop time, and fast-forward through the unpleasant or boring parts. As a result, he uses the remote to zip through uncomfortable moments for years, and only late in life does he realize that those seemingly bad moments he skipped over were actually some of the most meaningful times with his family, including his father's last days, while others were the moments he would have learned valuable life lessons.

In the end, the whole thing turns out to be a dream (sort of), but the lesson is clear: We don't know what moments of our lives will turn out to be significant, which ones will change who we are, and which will be the last moments we share with our loved ones. We should savor them all.

It's a ham-handed message delivered through a ridiculous premise, but it's a good analogy for the Swipe. By using the remote to click away from the parts of his life that he found tedious or frightening, Michael denied himself the full, rich human experience that makes life worth living. Swiping has the identical effect. In both cases, people disengage from any experience that isn't ideal, with unknowable consequences.

Psychological research supports the idea that it's the intense, sometimes negative experiences of our lives that give them depth and meaning. Researchers Sean Murphy and Brock Bastian found that extremity—the stress and emotional intensity of an experience, regardless of whether that emotion is positive or negative—correlates with the level of meaning people find in those experiences.[1] In other research, Paul Rozin found that engagement in activities ordinarily thought of as "sad" or "discomfiting," such as listening to sad music, watching scary movies, going on thrill rides, or eating painfully spicy food, actually gave many people pleasure.[2] While this is oversimplifying a bit, the takeaway from this and similar research can be summed up as follows:

Emotional extremes make us feel more alive.

It's the intensity of our experiences, not simply their positive-negative valence, that makes them enjoyable. While that enjoyment doesn't always occur in the moment, it arises upon reflection. The theory of posttraumatic growth, developed in the 1990s by psychologists Richard Tedeschi and Lawrence Calhoun, supports this idea. You might be terrified while riding a sky-high, hurtling roller coaster, but after the ride ends you're cackling with laughter, hair mussed and eyes glowing, feeling not only alive but thrilled. Because anger, grief, and fear tend to be our most intense emotions, some of our most meaningful experiences tend to be adverse: conflict, loss, risk.

Intense experiences become meaningful because of what psychologists call a *narrative identity perspective*. We construct the story of ourselves based on meaningful events we select from our lives. The more intense the event—and in many cases the greater the adversity we have to overcome to get through the event—the more we consider it to be self-defining. We call this the *storyteller's conceit*. The best stories from your life, the ones you'll share over a dinner with friends or around the fire on a camping trip, are almost always those in which everything went wrong: the time you got into a fight and spent the night in jail; the time your sailboat capsized in bad weather, and you almost drowned; the time your airline canceled all your flights, and you had to hitchhike to your best friend's wedding. We recount with both apprehension and pride how we slept for three days straight after putting in three consecutive seventy-hour weeks in order to knock out the work project everyone else had declared "impossible." Those are the stories that show you and others who you are, and they're also the most interesting. Nobody wants to listen to, "We went to Maui, it was awesome, and then we went home." We love adversity and triumph.

If extremity and intensity lend the events of our lives meaning, Swiping past them to gain a little transient comfort robs us of that meaning. The Swipe replaces the authentic experience with all its nuance—in effect, becomes the experience. Swiping has a personal cost to us all, and it may well be stunting our growth both as individuals and as a culture.

Swiping Changes How Others See You

There's no question that quitting something in a fit of pique or discomfort changes how you see yourself, and usually not for the better. "No one likes to fail, but some people take it harder than others," says mental health counselor Monte Drenner. "People with a healthy self-esteem tend to view failure as an event. People with low self-esteem often view failure as fatal. This thought process pummels one's self-esteem and overtime being a failure becomes their identity."[3]

This is one of the reasons many workplaces have changed their hiring practices to better identify candidates who are resilient and comfortable with VUCA (volatility, uncertainty, complexity, and ambiguity). VUCA-centric interview questions deviate markedly from more conventional questions, as popular prehire questions like these show:

- "Tell us about a time when things didn't go according to plan. Why was that the case, and what did you do about it?"

- "What have you accomplished, despite great difficulty, that you are particularly proud of and why?"
- "What life lessons did you gain through the COVID-19 period?"
- "Which smartphone app, if removed from your phone right now, would result in helping you be more successful than you are with that app installed?
- "What have you been working on for a long time that you are still struggling to complete or reach?"
- "How many golf balls can fit in a school bus?"

How many *what* can fit in a *what*? Who cares? These questions seem to provide greater insight into a candidate's thought process, view of failure, and propensity to engage or to Swipe, even when the answers are difficult or absent and the task becomes hard.

But consistently walking away from project after project, or from a life goal you insisted was everything, also affects how the people in your life perceive you. The mental image others construct of you is based largely on the consistency between your words and your actions. Do you do what you say you will do? Do you follow through on promises? In a nutshell, can you be trusted to be who you claim to be?

When you regularly embark on a challenging pursuit, and tell everyone about it, only to drop it like it's hot as soon as things get tough, you're sending multiple subtle but persuasive messages to the people in your circle:

- You don't know what you want.
- You crave the attention that comes with trying but don't want the disapproval and questions that come when you quit.
- You can't really commit.

- You aren't willing to gain the life experience that comes through stretching.
- You want the rewards but don't want to put in the work.

The last one can become problematic for friendships. After someone has watched you make an alleged commitment to something for the fifth time—"This time it will be different!"—only to Swipe once again, it's logical for that person to infer that if you can't commit to doing something that's clearly in your best interest, like losing weight or getting your college degree, maybe you're really not committed to the friendship either. We even have a word for people who can't seem to finish anything they start, who blunder about haplessly from one scheme to the next, always aflutter with grand intentions but forever tripping on their own flaws: *flake*.

The term came into popular slang in baseball as a reference to someone strange and eccentric, but it's become a pejorative for someone who can't be counted on. If one amusing pop culture definition of a *true friend* is "somebody who will come when you call at two in the morning, no questions asked, and bring gloves and a shovel," then the flake is the opposite of that—someone unreliable, someone who won't be there in a time of need. Nobody wants to be that person.

Still, the perception of being a flake, the guy or gal who never follows through, is still relatively harmless. Among your social circle, you might become the one everyone rolls their eyes at when you talk about finishing the novel you've been working on for nine years, or when you announce your ambitious New Year's resolution. No big deal, right? True, but what happens when consistently Swiping comes with higher stakes?

Swiping Corrodes Family Bonds

Visit Reddit and other online discussion boards, and you'll find endless laments by frustrated people about how their spouses seem unable to change their perceived laziness, their health, or their habits. This is a dimension of resentment and anger far beyond the simple "You're such a flake!" accusations we see thrown around between friends. In marriages and families, where individuals rely on one another to be dependable partners through thick and thin, consistently Swiping past commitments and the important work of self-improvement can eat away at familial bonds and eventually destroy families.

Suppose you are one of the approximately 50 percent of adults in the United States who try to lose weight every year.[4] Naturally, many of those people fail, which is why that percentage remains stubbornly high. But when the only thing at stake is your pride, there's little cost for Swiping, quitting, and then trying again when the newest fad diet pops up in your Twitter feed.

Quite simply, when you raise the stakes attached to something, whether it's improving your health, spending more time with family, getting your finances in order, getting a better job, or working on anger issues, you raise the expectations of those around you that you will be more committed to succeeding. *Of course he'll do it this time*, we tell ourselves, *because he knows how important this is to me*. And what stakes could be higher than the well-being of your family?

This belief, the *stakes fallacy*, gets the reasons behind Swiping wrong. The importance of a goal to yourself or someone else is no match for the reflexive reaction to discomfort that is the Swipe. Without real-time awareness of that neuropsychological mechanism at work, it doesn't matter how much you want to lose the weight or stop spending too much. Odds are, when push comes to shove, you'll revert to the same behavior patterns that have led to past failure.

When that happens, your spouse or children aren't thinking, *Well, you gave it your best shot, but some psychological barrier keeps getting in the way.* They're probably seething with frustration and even a sense of betrayal, thinking things like, *You're not committed, because you don't really care.* If you did care, you would get healthier, stick with your (or find a better) job, or keep seeing a therapist, right?

It's not difficult to see how these issues crush families. The Swipe compels parents to resist spending time with their children because it's easier to retreat into a world of video games or social media after a long day at work. It tempts them to run from those moments when they should lean in—those periods of difficulty over homework, dating, college, bullying, and other issues in which parents and kids can connect and grow together.

The famous Harry Chapin pop song "Cat's in the Cradle" perfectly illustrates this dilemma in warning us to better align our stated priorities with our actions. In the song, a father sings about his repeated failures to spend meaningful time with his son because of his work. At the end of the song, the father's refrain that his son was "gonna be like him" has come to pass: the son has grown into a man, with his own children and career, and now has no time for his father. It's a heartbreaking lesson.

In romantic partners, Swiping sparks avoidance of the tough conversations that can and should occur during a long relationship—about fidelity, communication, goals, and intimacy. The Swipe can shield family members from dealing with grief; prevent us from confronting life-or-death matters, like addiction or sexual abuse; and halt discussions of how to solve problems that are readily fixable but, if left unaddressed, can ruin a marriage. As Brené Brown writes:

When the people we love or with whom we have a deep connection stop caring, stop paying attention, stop investing and fighting for the relationship, trust begins to slip away and hurt starts seeping in. Disengagement triggers shame and our greatest fears—the fears of being abandoned, unworthy, and unlovable. What can make this covert betrayal so much more dangerous than something like a lie or an affair is that we can't point to the source of our pain—there's no event, no obvious evidence of brokenness. It can feel crazy-making.[5]

After all, no relationship expert has ever said, "The key to a healthy marriage is to avoid communicating at all costs."

NERD ALERT!

Disengagement as self-defense is a theory proposed by Canadian researchers, and it resonates with the Swipe. Their study found that older workers who felt their work was nonprestigious and unvalued by others shielded their self-esteem by devaluing that work themselves, treating their occupation as unimportant, and as a result making it less damaging to their self-image for others to look down upon it.[6] This form of defensive disengagement mirrors the disengagement of the Swipe, in which people reflexively withdraw from an activity when it becomes uncomfortably challenging, sparing their self-esteem the blow of outright failure. As with the Swipe, however, this worker disengagement was found to lead to decreases in self-esteem, casting doubt on the value of disengagement as a way to protect one's identity.

Swiping and FOMO

FOMO stands for fear of missing out—the state of envy and anxiety over the exciting, interesting lives you believe, often with scant evidence, your friends are leading while you toil away on the mundane and ordinary. It's an affliction of the social media age, made worse by people preening on Instagram and Facebook about their amazing travels, sumptuous meals, and other fabulous experiences. Never before have so many people gone out of their way to impress people they care so little about. And most of us fall into the trap of being influenced by those who have done nothing to deserve our interest or attention. FOMO pressures others to go beyond their dull, imperfect lives and match what their peers, or idols, are doing.

Getting out of your comfort zone is part of avoiding the Swipe, but there's a difference with FOMO. When you make a choice that's motivated by your anxiety over not doing what the "cool kids" appear to be doing, you're not making an affirmative decision to deal with discomfort and grow. You're desperately chasing the approval of other people—people you might not even know. There's nothing positive about that.

Acting on FOMO is simply another mechanism powering the Swipe. When someone elects to buy something or go somewhere in order to feel part of an influential tribe, they are falling victim to the "grass is always greener" sentiment that's at the heart of the Swipe. Never mind engaging more with your current job, or discovering hidden wonders in the city you live in—it's far more exciting to pull up stakes and move to Thailand or to hand in your resignation to go to Burning Man. All the cool kids are doing it! Unfortunately, any high from such peak experiences is fleeting, as such choices come from a place of fear and envy, the terror of being left out of the club. They're borrowed dreams.

Inevitably, the person driven by FOMO finds the experience isn't transformational at all. They're the same after Coachella or living on a kibbutz as they were before. The exultation fades and becomes more of that familiar "What have I done?" dread. Meanwhile, the life, career, and people left in the wake of the FOMO decision are still there, stunned and forgotten, eventually moving on.

The FOMO version of the Swipe also comes with real costs. A study of 1,045 Americans aged eighteen to thirty-four, conducted by personal finance company Credit Karma, found that nearly 40 percent had gone into debt to keep up with their friends' lifestyles, spending money they didn't have primarily on clothing, electronics, food, travel, and alcohol.[7] That's a kind of Swipe double jeopardy: turn your back on your authentic life to keep up with the millennial Joneses and rack up credit card debt doing it, only to find that you wind up right back where you started—anxious and unhappy.

As author Sherri Gordon writes, "The problem is that incessant worrying about what everyone else is doing only causes teens to miss out on their own lives even more. In fact, FOMO causes people to keep their attention focused outward instead of inward. This, in turn, may cause them to lose their sense of identity and to struggle with low self-esteem. But worse yet, when they are struggling with FOMO, that means they are so focused on what others are doing that they forget to live their own lives."[8]

The Swipe and Mental Health

As you might expect, the pressures brought on by Swiping can have a powerful impact on our mental health and well-being. Writers from the *New York Times* to *Psychology Today* have fretted in recent years about the rise in anxiety among young people, and most of that hand-wringing occurred before the pandemic that locked us all in our rooms with only our computers and phones for company. Psychotherapist Amy Morin points out that one reason for the spike in anxiety among teens is the easy escape from emotions offered by electronics—the Swipe in a nutshell.

"Constant access to digital devices lets kids escape uncomfortable emotions like boredom, loneliness, or sadness by immersing themselves in games when they are in the car or by chatting on social media when they are sent to their rooms," she writes. "And now we're seeing what happens when an entire generation has spent their childhoods avoiding discomfort. Their electronics replaced opportunities to develop mental strength, and they didn't gain the coping skills they need to handle everyday challenges."[9]

A recent study looked at the impact of technology on emotional regulation. The study involved 269 toddlers (two-to-three-year-olds). The question the researchers were looking to address was whether putting technology in the hands of a toddler in order to keep the toddler from having a tantrum had any effect on the child. The resulting article, appropriately titled "Tantrums, Toddlers, and Technology," found that problematic media use had significant impact on the child's ability to control his or her emotions. The researchers issued a clear warning to parents to avoid using media as a primary way to regulate children's emotion.[10] In other words, parents, stop putting the iPad in your kid's hand anytime he or she is screaming—it will only make matters worse in the long run.

But that's just scratching the surface of the Swipe's impact on mental health. While Swiping can impair the development of healthy coping skills by keeping people of all ages from confronting conditions like depression and anxiety, it can also contribute to them. When either physical or mental Swiping becomes habitual, it's easy over a period of years to internalize failure, to personalize it, as seen in pioneering psychologist Martin Seligman's doctrine of learned helplessness. When we try and fail over and over again, we can become fatalistic, convinced "things will never change for me." Given enough time, some of us come to believe that not only can we not make meaningful changes in our lives but that we are *unworthy* of change. From that place of bleak hopelessness, it's a short jump to the idea that life has no meaning or value, leading to depressive disorders and even suicidal ideations.

We can see the effects of this self-induced impotence in society today. A Harvard Youth Poll of 2,513 Americans aged eighteen to twenty-nine released in May 2021 found that 51 percent of them said they felt down, depressed, or hopeless.[11] Buffeted by a seemingly endless health crisis, political violence, inexorable climate change, and a rough economy, we seem to be losing our resilience, in great part because we've denied ourselves the opportunity to strive—to prove that we have the fortitude to survive and thrive under tough circumstances. Instead, more of us are feeling cynical, helpless, and hopeless.

One of the fundamental tenets of mental health is that a problem that remains unconfronted remains unresolved. Having built a culture that enables us to easily Swipe away from our fears and difficulties, we're now trapped in a feedback loop in which failure—and the inability to face that failure, learn from it, and rise above it—leads to debilitating emotions and more failure.

That's the flow in which mental health issues also *cause* the Swipe. We're in a bull market for overwhelm, anxiety, and depression, all of which can lead to the "I give up" mentality characteristic of the Swipe. "Depression is one of the principal causes," says licensed clinical social worker Cynthia Catchings. "It typically creates a lack of motivation and deep sadness that prevents the person from seeing beyond that. Anxiety can be a common cause as well. The fear of doing something, and what can happen if we do it, makes some people want to give up before even trying." Catchings says that posttraumatic stress disorder can also lead to this mindset. "PTSD can also fall under this category," she says. "Many symptoms affect the person when this diagnosis is present, causing him or her to feel like giving up. Some of these symptoms are fear, panic attacks, sadness, low self-esteem, and negative cognitions."[12]

Finally, the impulse to Swipe can also cause us to disengage from getting help with mental illness. According to the report *Mental Health Has Bigger Challenges Than Stigma*, from the Mental Health Million Project, 45 percent of people in the United States with a mental health issue requiring clinical intervention don't seek professional help.[13] That's hardly surprising when we consider the stigma associated with mental illness, together with the fact that millions of people with mental illness cannot access treatment due to inadequate health insurance or resources. It's more pleasurable to distract ourselves from dealing with the reality of anxiety, panic, depression, or addiction than it is to engage in the slow, grueling work of talk therapy, self-discovery, and recovery. So these problems fester and grow in millions, and society becomes ever sicker—and perversely, more likely to Swipe away from what we can't bear to look at. The feedback loop keeps running.

HOW NOT TO SWIPE

Having a strong motivation behind your goal, project, or dream is a proven effective way to reduce the chances of quitting in a moment of panic. One reason many endeavors end up as Swipes is because the motivation behind them is weak or vague. Often this occurs because people assume motivation is self-evident. Many times it is not. Instead, we need to examine what our motivation truly is and determine if that motivation is sufficient to propel us through the most difficult parts of the experience. Simply saying, "I've always wanted to be fit," will rarely be as strong a motivating force for engaging in an intense weight-loss program as something like, "If I lose thirty pounds, I can get off blood pressure medication." Understanding the "why" is more important than understanding the "what."

Veronica Hanson of Vacay Visionary has a unique approach to motivation. "People who are properly motivated will do what needs to be done every time," she wrote in our email interview. "If someone is not finishing what they start, it's because they aren't connected to the real reason why they want to accomplish the thing they ultimately quit. There are three levels of desire that can unlock your ultimate motivation. Level-one desire is anything you would be willing to say out loud to someone asking you what you aspire to have or do in life. Things we are willing to say out loud are superficial and heavily controlled by expectations of others, whether we admit it or not. Level-two desires are the ideas we let live in our heads and daydream about on a regular basis. Our daydream-level desires only go as deep as what we have allowed ourselves to believe we are worthy of, which is often much less than we truly deserve. Finally, level-three desires are the ideas that as soon as they enter your brain you immediately kick the idea in the face. You tell yourself it's ridiculous to even bother imagining that insanity because it will never realistically happen. These desires are the only ones that will truly drive the action necessary to change behavior. To finish what you start, you must unlock your deepest desires."

Swiping and the Death of Empathy

Swiping doesn't just impact us on a personal level. It's also partially responsible for the modern escalation in vitriol, intolerance, and rage we see so often in today's news. From attacks on school board members to violent threats against election officials to the coarsening of public discourse, society seems to have devolved into a frontier of armed camps, each conditioned to see the other as an absolute, implacable enemy—to be viewed not only with suspicion but with seething hatred. Outrage has become currency. It brings attention, eyeballs, and clicks. Outrage generates revenue and political donations. If it's corrosive to the common good, oh well.

This sad state of affairs is part of what *Scientific American* called the *empathy deficit*.[14] Today, more so than in any time in recent memory, people throughout the world seem crippled in their ability to grasp the challenges other people face or find sympathy for their pain and hardship. We seem indifferent to the needs of others and concerned primarily with our own selfish whims, even if those whims are irrational or detrimental to the well-being of people who are supposed to be our brothers and sisters.

Technology has played an important role in getting us to this precarity. Yes, it's easy to blame social media for making it easy for us to cocoon ourselves into epistemic bubbles of information and opinion that only serve to confirm our existing biases and feed our fears. But that's not the only reason for the decay of our civic engagement and mutual respect. In part because of the COVID-19 pandemic, but also because we choose to engage with one another at a distance via technology—*engagement lite*, we might call it— we're not as adept at reading nonverbal cues or picking up on perspectives that might differ from our own. Our empathy seems to be atrophying.

That makes us less likely to care about the people who hold opposing views—partly because it never really gives us time to consider their opinions—and more likely to Swipe away from them. Humans are naturally tribal, and when it becomes difficult, even unpleasant, to try and comprehend beliefs that might be in opposition to our own, we quit trying. Things that are hard yield their rewards grudgingly, but when we understand the views of someone who thinks like we do, the rewards are immediate: approval, a sense of belonging, even higher status within the tribe. That's why *virtue signaling*, words or acts that display a tribally approved set of values, is such a popular pastime.

In 2012 Hurricane Sandy slammed into the East Coast of the United States, causing a near-complete loss of power and internet service in a wide part of the region. Researchers used this event as an opportunity to explore the effect of the sudden and complete withdrawal of technology on people's emotions and behavior. After periods ranging from a few days to several weeks, participants in the study said they were more mindful, especially in their relationships.[15] While much of this mindfulness surely can be attributed to gratitude and renewed appreciation for these relationships under these difficult circumstances, the researchers found that the absence of technology for a short period removed some of the distraction that hindered these relationships under normal circumstances. Technology, while it is troubling in its own way, is merely an enabler of Swiping. It isn't what makes us Swipe.

Remember: The Swipe is an automatic reaction to discomfort, not a deliberate, conscious choice. When confronted by opinions or views that are radically, even offensively, different from our own, we would take the opportunity to quickly disengage from them rather than try to comprehend their origins and the people who hold them. We are confirmation machines. We adore having our biases confirmed because it makes us feel intelligent, virtuous, even superior. In the face of such positive stimuli, the prospect of standing firm and feeling empathy for the guy on the other side of the politico-philosophical fence doesn't stand a chance.

Empathy is disincentivized, while tribalism encourages us to Swipe to what we know and who we trust. After a while our empathy muscles atrophy, and we wind up where we are now.

Is There Anything Positive about Swiping?

That's a lot of doom and gloom. It's important to understand that there is hope! Life doesn't have to be one Swipe after another. But is there anything beneficial about the Swipe? That depends on your viewpoint. For instance, what is now known internationally as the Great Resignation, the mass exodus of people from their jobs in the wake of the pandemic, was hailed as an inflection point for self-empowerment in the labor movement. That may be, when you consider the millions who have quit grueling, low-status, poorly paying jobs in search of greater work-life balance and more respect. In that context, quitting something is laudatory. But we would argue that the Great Resignation is not a Swipe en masse.

Swiping is reactionary, not logical and considered. Deciding to leave your job because you feel unappreciated, undercompensated, stagnant, and burned out is a rational process that plays out over time, involving executive function and one's sense of identity and self-worth. Even if it's driven largely by emotion, it's not a reflex. The employees walking out of Burger Kings and Dollar Generals from coast to coast are doing so from an affirmative sense that they can find better, not the impulse to dodge discomfort. In fact, they're *choosing* the discomfort of an uncertain income because their self-respect demands it.

There's only one potential real benefit from Swiping. Since a true Swipe is a fight-or-flight act, it could possibly get you out of a situation in which you're in physical, psychological, or financial danger. But that's about it.

That positive impact is limited by the behavioral strictures of the Swipe. Even if we discover new paths, if we're prone to Swipe when challenge becomes uncomfortably great, we're going to keep doing it with new activities, just as we did with the old ones. The same pattern of panic, leading to abandonment and disengagement, leading to regret and self-recrimination, continues. As we'll see, that's true not only in our personal lives but in our professional lives as well.

CHAPTER 4

Disengaged: The Swipe at Work

When someone's uncomfortable or bored on the job, Swiping means quitting as a reactive impulse. But that can result in lost opportunity, self-sabotage, and harm to the organization as well as the employee. There's a solution: MAGIC.

In 2016 the *Guardian* published a story titled "Long Lunch: Spanish Civil Servant Skips Work for Years Without Anyone Noticing." The article began as follows: "Only when Joaquín García, a Spanish civil servant, was due to collect an award for two decades of loyal and dedicated service did anyone realize that he had not, in fact, shown up to work for at least 6 years – and possibly as many as 14."

Garcia was an engineer hired to supervise a wastewater treatment plant in Cádiz, Spain. It wasn't until he was to receive an award for his lengthy service and dedication that the deputy mayor who had originally hired Garcia tried to track down the man. As the deputy mayor inquired of coworkers, including the former manager of the water board, he found that nobody had seen Garcia for years. The deputy mayor called the engineer to inquire about what he had been working on. Garcia was unable to answer.

A court fined Garcia the equivalent of one year's salary. They found he "had not been in his office for at least six years," and that he "had done absolutely no work between 2007 and 2010, the year before he retired."

Garcia admitted to the court that he "may not have kept regular business hours." The court concluded that the water board had assumed Garcia was working under the direction of the city council, while the city council believed Garcia had been answering to the water board. It was like something out of a Hollywood screwball comedy. The *Guardian* reported that Garcia had "made the most of the confusion, becoming an avid reader of philosophy" and becoming an expert in the works of the Dutch philosopher Spinoza.[1]

We can't help wondering how we go about getting a gig like that. Okay, granted, this sounds a lot more like a dishonest employee than it does a Swipe, but stay with us for a moment. When we, along with Matthew Wride, wrote the book *The Employee Experience* in 2017, we found we were entering what we referred to as the "Age of the Employee." Historically, the employer-employee relationship has been adversarial. Companies have regarded employees as necessary liabilities, and in turn, employees assumed organizations would exploit them in any way they could in order to bolster profits. Armed with the power of the pink slip, companies had the upper hand.

During the past couple of decades, however, there has been a shift in power. We are now in an era in which employees have more choices and power than ever before. "Help Wanted" signs have proliferated like dandelions. If an employee's needs (and wants) are not met where they work today, they can head for the exits and probably have multiple job offers in a matter of days.

As we began the research for our book *The Employee Experience* in 2016, we found that 50 percent of US workers were thinking about making a career change, even if it wasn't immediate.[2] Now, coming on the heels of the global COVID-19 pandemic, worldwide resignations, or "quits," are at an all-time high, and we're not just talking about recent college grads, as one might suspect. *Harvard Business Review* reports that an analysis of more than nine million employee records at four thousand global companies found that while turnover is still highest among younger employees resignations for employees between thirty and forty-five years old increased by an average of 20 percent in 2021.

Not surprisingly, resignations in the health-care and technology sectors spiked, partly due to the increased pressure brought on by the pandemic.[3] We have now entered the Great Resignation, and the number of currently employed job seekers is on the rise. Those are the facts, but what are the implications? What does this have to do with the Swipe? Let's go there.

Here We Go Again

The Great Resignation is not a new phenomenon. Employees have been disengaging from their work for as long as there has *been* work. Has this problem become more pronounced over the past decade? Perhaps, but what we might call the "Job Swipe" has been around for a long time.

Sometime around 100 BC, Roman general and statesman Gaius Marius restructured the Roman army. Citizens joining the army would serve for between sixteen and twenty years, and all Roman men between the ages of seventeen and forty-six could be called up to serve in the army. The army was organized into legions of six thousand men, each commanded by a senator, called a *legatus*. Of the six thousand, only fifty-three hundred would be specifically tasked with combat. The rest were charged with supportive noncombat roles: messengers, builders, clerks, surveyors, water engineers, musicians, blacksmiths, surgeons, and weapon makers.

Being assigned to the front didn't always mean constant action, however. For extended periods during the rule of the Roman Empire, the Romans were not at war. In these times, even soldiers assigned to combat might spend months or years guarding slaves in mines or building roads, forts, and waterways. This was certainly not duty rich with the glamour, honor, and fame associated with fighting for the empire.

Because of the often mundane nature of their duties, as well as human nature, even disciplined Roman soldiers were guilty of checking out or disengaging from time to time. The punishments for this were severe. If a solider was found guilty of falling asleep on duty or leaving his post, he could be punished by a process known as *fustuarium*. Fellow soldiers were required to club or stone the soldier, which usually resulted in death. If groups deserted their posts, the punishment was equally brutal.[4] But commanders knew that if they executed all the men from a given post, they would be left without enough men to fight. Instead, they chose one-tenth of the deserters at random and set an example for the others by clubbing the smaller group to death.[5] This process of losing or destroying one-tenth of group gave us the term *decimation* (from the Latin *decem*, meaning "ten").

Different era, same story. Disengagement and resignation are with us today. Fortunately for those who find it difficult to be fully engaged in their work, there are three major differences between the employee of two thousand years ago and that of today:

- While employee abuse certainly does occur, workers today generally don't have to fear for their lives if they need an hour away for a medical appointment or miss a meeting due to illness or other factors.
- Employers are far more aware of what is known today as the employee experience, or EX. The experience employees have with the organization has a clear impact on their levels of engagement. EX is the sum of perceptions employees have about their interactions with their organizations.[6] Employers today recognize the fact that the employee experience is directly related to the success of the organization. Rather than being considered a necessary evil, employers understand that employees *are* the organization.
- Finally, a dissatisfied Roman soldier would have a difficult time resigning from his role and picking up a job with the Persian army because he "didn't really like his job." But in the Age of the Employee, with far more jobs available today than bodies to fill them, today's dissatisfied employee can likely find a new job easily.

NERD ALERT!

A *legatus* in the Roman army was the equivalent of a high-ranking general. After a military campaign, officers would receive large shares of the military's bounty, making this a very lucrative and sought-after position.[7]

The term *legatus* eventually made its way into the English language as *legate*, from which came the verb "to delegate" (the prefix meaning "away from oneself"), meaning to choose someone to do something you don't want to do.

What Is Engagement, Anyway?

What hasn't changed is the fact that we all disengage from our work at some point. For more than twenty years, we have studied the concept of employee engagement. We have worked with hundreds of organizations and tens of thousands of leaders to understand what creates engagement in the workplace. We've gathered lots and lots of data about what causes individuals in any organization to disengage.

We've already talked about engagement in this book, but just what is it? To engage is to participate in or become involved in something. We are engaged by activities that capture our attention and interest. To be precise:

Engagement is an emotional state in which we feel passionate, energetic, and committed to our work. In turn, we fully invest our best selves—our hearts, spirits, minds, and hands—in the work we do.

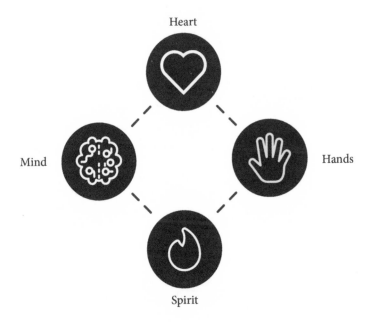

Heart

Mind   Hands

Spirit

Heart is about finding meaning, passion, fulfillment, and even joy in what you do. *Spirit* is about the attitude, energy, and excitement you can feel when you walk into a room or work with a terrific team. Heart and spirit imply that we must *feel* the work that we do.

But in order to be fully engaged, we must act. That's where the mind and hands come in. *Mind* is about intellect, interests, curiosity, and creativity. *Hands* are about effort, productivity, and self-determination—using your skills and sweat to produce something of value.[8]

The benefit of engagement to any organization should be clear. Engagement shows up in a company's bottom line as increased profitability, greater productivity, improved efficiencies, and higher quality. We also see its presence in decreased turnover, improved employee satisfaction, reduced employee-related legal expenses, safety, and general loyalty.

Endless books and articles have been written about the advantages of engagement for the organization and its leaders. But why should an employee want to get on board with the whole engagement thing? An employee might quite reasonably say, "I can see why my being engaged with my job helps my company. But what's in it for me?" It's a good question.

Besides the fact that we all have an inherent need to be engaged, our research reveals clear reasons every one of us, from the C-suite to the cubicle dweller to the part-time work-from-homer, should *want* to be engaged at work. Based on our analysis of more than one hundred thousand survey responses, supported by numerous studies, there are sound personal reasons why everyone should want to be engaged on the job:[9]

1. **Better health.** One study monitored a group of 168 engaged and disengaged workers at various intervals during a day to measure stress and other health factors. Engaged workers reported lower stress levels throughout the day. They also showed improvements in cholesterol and blood pressure readings. Conversely, disengaged employees were twice as likely to be diagnosed with depression as those who were engaged.[10]

2. **Happiness.** Employee engagement and happiness are closely related but are not necessarily the same. Employees can be happy yet not fully engaged in their work, and vice versa; however, those who are fully engaged in what they do are more likely to say they are happy. Additionally, those who are happy are 12 percent more productive than those who

aren't.[11] According to Shawn Achor, Harvard professor and author of *The Happiness Advantage*, "When we are positive, our brains become more engaged, creative, motivated, energetic, resilient, and productive at work." Happy employees are nearly ten times more engaged in their work than their disengaged counterparts.

3. **Productivity, pay, and advancement.** Engaged employees not only work harder but also work smarter and are able to produce better results than their less engaged peers. This results in higher wages, faster promotions, and the ability for those employees to market themselves for better career opportunities. According to Achor, when you are happy in your work, your productivity increases by 31 percent, and you're 40 percent more likely to receive a promotion.

4. **Better home life.** Best of all, workplace benefits don't mean sacrificing work-life balance. Being fully engaged at work allows you to get more out of home life too. DecisionWise research shows that engaged employees are far more likely to be engaged outside work as well. Also, according to Achor, when you are engaged in life in general, you live longer, get better grades, experience less severe symptoms of illness, and are generally more content with life.

While some of these reasons might resonate with you, only you can decide if you should or shouldn't engage in your job. It's a pretty important decision. After all, you spend at least one-third of your waking hours at work. Would you rather spend that significant chunk of your life engaged with your work or cynical, discouraged, and Swiping?

Why Engagement Matters

At nearly every conference we attend and in every article we read about employee engagement, we encounter a statistic like this: "Seventy-eight percent of employees are disengaged and unlikely to make a positive contribution to their workplace."

Do I really need to walk past seven employees in the hall before I finally pass one who cares about their job? Why not just fire the 78 percent and let the remaining 22 percent do the work? We could even pay them more! As with most things, the truth isn't that simple.

We've explored two decades of research done by employee experience firm DecisionWise. The firm's database on the topic is immense, with more than fifty million employee survey responses. We learned a great deal from these responses. First, the notion that more than three-quarters of us are disengaged from our jobs is nonsense. Could an organization even function if 78 percent of its head count had checked out without telling anyone? Not a chance. Plus, most of us *want* to engage in what we do. We want to enjoy our work, to find meaning and satisfaction in it. It's not our nature to wake up in the morning saying, "I hope today stinks."

Second, because of the belief that the vast majority of employees are disengaged, US companies spend about $2 billion a year trying to "drive engagement" or to "get employees engaged" and to solve the engagement dilemma. Most aren't getting much return for their investment. Finally, while engagement is largely personal—what makes us disengage might not make you disengage—there are some commonalities. It turns out that five factors—we refer to them by the acronym MAGIC—must be present in order for people to engage in their work. More on those later.

Our most important finding was that when one or more of these keys is absent, especially in a workplace setting, people are extremely likely to Swipe. And just as the Swipe in our personal lives leads to lost opportunity, regret, and unhappiness, the Swipe in our professional lives has a similar effect. What's more, the workplace Swipe not only affects us as individuals but it affects the organization to which we belong and our professional colleagues.

Why does all this matter? Because most of us will spend one-third to one-half of our waking hours at work. For the average US adult, that equates to about *one-fourth of our lives*. Plus, work is not just where we earn a paycheck. It's often the center of our social relationships, the linchpin of our identities, and the venue where we turn our aspirations and ambitions into realities, like inventions and companies.

Thus, when employees become disengaged and Swipe at their jobs, they harm not only their professional prospects but their personal lives, the well-being of the colleagues who depend on them, the stability of the organizations they work for, and even the economy. Engagement, disengagement, and the Swipe are prime movers of business, economic activity, and careers. Understanding how the Swipe works is key to reducing employee disengagement and avoiding the damage the Swipe can inflict upon workers' lives and futures.

Also, our research shows us that those who Swipe in the workplace are more likely to do so in other environments as well, whether that means turning away from important moments with family or dropping important personal goals. If we are disengaging in our work lives, odds are we are disengaging in other areas, whether we admit it or not.

BOO!

In the dating world, ghosting refers to the practice of abruptly ending a relationship without contact, communication, explanation, or warning. Well, ghosting has now entered the workplace as well.

Workplace ghosting shares some commonalities with the dating world, with employees and potential employees going silent without explanation. This includes not showing for a scheduled interview, no-showing on the first day of work, or quitting without notice.

Ghosting is a two-way street. Employers are often guilty of ghosting potential hires. This occurs when a job candidate applies for a job but is not contacted by the employer, or when the candidate goes through the hiring process—interview, providing references, etc.—but does not hear back from the company. Interestingly, 41 percent of job seekers believe it is more reasonable for applicants to ghost companies than for companies to ghost applicants (32 percent).

Can we all just agree it's 100 percent disrespectful, in any relationship, regardless of who ghosts and who gets ghosted?

Does Quitting Equal Swiping?

When you add up all these facts and factor in the ennui and cynicism that lies behind much of the Great Resignation, it appears that employees at every level are indeed Swiping at their jobs. They're disengaging, walking away, and souring on even the concept of work, at least temporarily. But that's anecdotal evidence. Do we have data?

Let us say right now that quitting your job isn't always the wrong option. It may very well be the right choice. But is that choice the result of a thoughtful decision or a reactive Swipe? New evidence shows it may be the latter.

Studies published in 2021 by researchers Meike Sons and Cornelia Niessen detailed the results of a study of 2,565 workers, including 1,574 working parents who had left jobs for other work. They found that in these newfound jobs satisfaction and overall vitality (energy) *declined* for the first year and slightly beyond. The sense of belonging and fit within the new organization also dropped. The researchers also discovered that work-family conflict climbed sharply when an employee switched jobs.[12]

According to a survey by recruiting platform Jobvite, 30 percent of employees leave their jobs within the first ninety days of getting hired in a new role. Of those, 43 percent said their role didn't match their expectation of the job. Another 34 percent reported there was a specific incident that caused them to leave. Thirty-two percent blamed company culture and fit.[13]

Data found by DecisionWise indicates a similar phenomenon. In studying over one hundred thousand new hires across various organizations, we found that engagement in the workplace tends to be highest for employees who are in the organization for one year or less—more specifically, over the first six months. This is often referred to in the workplace as the "honeymoon period." From years two to four of employment, engagement wanes, dropping an average of 20 percent from that of the new hires. Then, strangely, engagement levels for employees who stay with an organization for five years or more tend to rise again and even surpass that of the one-year-or-less group.

Is this because all workplaces are bad? Obviously not, or

declines in engagement would correlate with the time someone was employed at an organization. Do organizations change their cultures every six months? Of course not. Instead, we turn to a story that may help illustrate the psychology at play here.

A colleague of ours is a psychologist who runs a successful counseling practice. Several of the therapists in his employ meet regularly with young people regarding their romantic relationships. In describing why they can't find lasting relationships, these young counselees share variations of a common phrase: "I always seem to date weirdos." As these counselors work to turn the conversation back to the individual, rather than on the people around the individual, they also work to help their patients accept the harsh truth: the only common denominator in their never-ending chain of bad relationships is *them*.

In the words of either meditation writer Jon Kabat-Zinn or the movie *The Adventures of Buckaroo Banzai*, "Wherever you go, there you are."

In this the Age of the Employee, employees have choices like never before. Over the past several years, social media has added fuel to the fire, with opinion posts from those claiming that remaining with an organization for more than eighteen months is a sign the person in question either isn't marketable, fears change, or is too lazy to look for another gig. Most of these posts come from those who ricochet from job to job, and who appear to be looking for validation for their own situation by dragging others down with them. Mix in endless distractions from technology and the existential nature of the COVID-19 pandemic, and voilà, you get the Swipe—a Great Resignation cocktail, shaken and not stirred.

Why Employees Disengage

People sour on a job for as many different reasons as there are people: poor pay, management disrespect, work-life imbalance, boredom, and a thousand other causes. As we completed research for the book *Engagement MAGIC* in 2019, however, we discovered that engagement is a fifty-fifty proposition, meaning that the organization has a responsibility to create the environment in which employees can choose to engage. But as we pointed out in a previous chapter, in the end, engagement is a *choice*—the employee's choice. It's up to the organization to till the soil and lay down the nutrients that allow people the opportunity to put down roots, but it's up to the employee to do so or not.

You've heard the phrase "People join companies but leave managers," right? Our database of more than fifty million employee survey responses supports that idea. In fact, when employees have a negative perception of their manager, they will leave the company 56 percent more often than employees who hold their manager in high regard. Also, when a manager is fully engaged at work, a whopping 87 percent more of that manager's direct reports are fully engaged than in a company in which the manager isn't fully engaged. So, yes, managers make a *big* difference. But they don't make all the difference.

Social media titan Meta (formerly Facebook) found that its employees were indeed more likely to jump ship when the boss was horrible; however, most respondents to their study indicated they had pretty good bosses. The decision to run for the exits was because they didn't like the work, not the boss.

Perhaps even more interesting was that when Meta's people analytics team reviewed employee survey data to predict who would stay or leave their jobs over the next six months they learned something important about those who chose to stay. Those likely to remain found their work enjoyable 31 percent more often, said the work used their strengths 33 percent more often, and expressed 37 percent more confidence that they were gaining skills that would help them in their future careers than the folks who left.[14]

Organizational psychologist, author, and Wharton business school professor Adam Grant suggests that, just as romantic relationships have deal-breakers, perhaps work relationships should have them as well.[15] He says that instead of making the decision to quit a job on impulse or reflex—and also when they might be angry or emotional—employees starting a new job should make a list of factors that—should they occur—would make them want to quit. The alternative is to leave one organization because we don't belong, only to spend the next six months not belonging in our next organization.

Why You Should Care about Employees Swiping

If you're an employer or a supervisor, you might be saying, "So what? Sure, I don't love having to replace people all the time, but if my disengaged employees Swipe and give their notice, they're doing me a favor. What's the big deal?" The big deal is that it's not the employees who Swipe and leave who you have to worry about. It's the ones who Swipe and *don't* leave. They are the ones who can sabotage your entire organization.

The origins of the word *sabotage* are murky. Some believe it has a connection to a French word for shoe, *sabot*. One version has it that the word derives from the fifteenth century, when disgruntled Dutch workers would throw their wooden shoes into the mills or textile looms in order to bring textile manufacturing to a standstill. Other versions suggest that *sabotage* comes from nineteenth-century French slang for an unskilled peasant laborer who did poor-quality work; these laborers often wore wooden shoes.

Regardless of the origins, the basic meaning of the word holds true: causing harm or undermining a cause, usually in secret. We typically associate sabotage with the destruction of an organization, a structure like a bridge, or a vessel like a ship or aircraft.

Sabotage has often been viewed as both noble and justified. *The Simple Sabotage Field Manual*,[16] produced in 1944 by the US Office of Strategic Services (the precursor to the CIA), instructed US citizens in ways to sabotage domestic factories and other industries should America fall under the control of either Nazi Germany or the Soviet Union. Though written over seven decades ago, the instructions appear strangely applicable to modern organizations:

- **Managers and Supervisors:** To lower morale and production, be pleasant to inefficient workers; give them undeserved promotions. Discriminate against efficient workers; complain unjustly about their work.
- **Employees:** Work slowly. Think of ways to increase the number of movements needed to do your job: use a light hammer instead of a heavy one; try to make a small wrench do, instead of a big one.
- **Organizations and Conferences:** When possible, refer all matters to committees for "further study and consideration." Attempt to make the committees as large and bureaucratic as possible. Hold conferences when there is more critical work to be done.
- **Telephone:** At office, hotel, and local telephone switchboards, delay putting calls through, give out wrong numbers, cut

people off "accidentally," or forget to disconnect them so that the line cannot be used again.

- **Transportation:** Make train travel as inconvenient as possible for enemy personnel. Issue two tickets for the same seat on a train in order to set up an "interesting" argument.

Disengaged employees do sabotage an organization's progress, but this is fairly uncommon. According to our research, fewer than 4 percent of employees are actively disengaged, and most of those employees either resign or face termination. Far more common is the employee who commits "passive sabotage." These are those employees who have Swiped—who are bitter, world-weary, and frustrated—but who do just enough to keep their jobs.

These employees simply don't care. They may not actively be looking for ways to destroy the organization, but their hearts and heads aren't in the game. They may not report a quality concern when they notice one. They may refuse to go the extra mile for the customer, take longer than needed to get the job done, tune out in meetings, or balk at training the new hire. They're the people who do the minimum and then clock out. Our research has found that roughly 16 percent of employees fit into this category. Even though their intentions might not be to harm or hamper, the outcome of their indifference is often the same as if they were actively trying to cause harm. They are often not even aware they are saboteurs, nor would they consider what they are doing sabotage—they just don't care anymore.[17]

Self-Sabotage

What if you're not the employer, but the employee? You could be saying, "I'm not a saboteur. What does this have to do with me?"

More than you might think. You may not believe you are guilty of workplace sabotage, but if you're habitually Swiping in your creative life, your romantic relationships, or your personal growth goals, you might also be Swiping on the job. The tricky part is that sabotage is often passive. You may have disengaged, checked out, and stopped caring, but at the same time you are convinced you're a decent employee. *I'm not employee of the month or anything, but I take care of business.* But what if you don't?

We've worked with thousands of businesses and hundreds of thousands of employees, and most of them would never call themselves saboteurs. They wouldn't dream of introducing malicious code into the company's computer network or screaming profanities at an important customer. What many of us don't realize is that sabotage isn't always something we do to an organization or to other people. When you stop caring about your work, when you don't give your best, when you quit a good job out of panic or discomfort, you don't just hurt your company. You deny yourself chances to grow, learn, and advance.

Why? Well, while many of us self-sabotage in our personal lives—undermining our efforts to learn a new language, for example, or texting that old flame we swore we'd never see again—our work lives are different. In your personal life, you're the boss. You don't answer to anyone else, and you can delude yourself into thinking that if you walk away from something you care about you can always come back to it again later. But at work, you're not the boss. You're serving many masters, from your customers to your supervisor to the CEO or president of the organization. If you're an educator, you're serving your students and their parents. In health care, it's the patients. Under those circumstances, with many people making many demands on your energy and time, disengaging and sabotaging can feel less like failure and more like striking back at the Man. If your district manager is an arrogant jerk, what better way to get back at her than fall short of your sales numbers so she looks bad?

The trouble is, you're not just hurting the Man.

In the moment, most self-sabotage doesn't look like sabotage. It's not until we look back that we see we are undermining our own success.

"Self-sabotage isn't sabotage at all," explains psychotherapist Shirani Pathak. "It's actually a protective mechanism created by your psyche in order to keep you safe from any potential danger or harm. What's familiar to us is what our psyche considers safe." You may not even be aware of self-sabotaging behavior, and it isn't something you do on purpose.[18]

Workplace sabotage often overlaps with self-sabotage. If you're a part of that 50 percent of the workforce who are shopping their résumés, you aren't only Swiping to escape discomfort. You're also actively disengaged from your organization and the people in it.

Let's take a look at how the same Swiping scenario might be destructive to both an organization and to an individual:

Sabotaging the Organization's Success	Sabotaging Your Own Success
You hang up on a customer without solving a problem because they are difficult to work with.	You haven't put your training to use. You have missed the opportunity to build a relationship and aren't getting noticed.
Vandals break out the windows of a nearby school while you watch from your apartment but choose not to get involved.	You feel guilty for your inaction each day you look out your apartment window and see plywood covering the windows.
You don't deliver your portion of the critical group project due at school, leaving others to do it for you.	Not only are you not a "team player" but you haven't contributed your unique talents. You don't learn the assigned material.
While your child is telling you about how she stood up for a bullied friend at school, your mind drifts off to your work.	You have wasted a precious opportunity to build this key family relationship, recognize your child, and help her grow.
You are out to dinner with your significant other, and you constantly check your text messages rather than communicating.	The relationship continues to decline. You aren't happy, because you "don't talk anymore." Nobody is having fun.
You quit your job after nine months. Your company has invested six months in training you.	You have only been a contributor for the past three months. Your résumé screams "short-timer." You've gained few, if any, new skills.

We all know someone who doesn't seem to last more than a year at any job. The one who left their last job because the boss wasn't flexible with their childcare situation. Before that, it was the company where there was no growth potential. Before that came the one-year Himalayan spirit quest, the company that didn't pay what they were worth, and the coworkers who were idiots.

Seeing a pattern? Sure, there are legitimate reasons to quit a gig. Giving two-weeks' notice might even be the best option. But when you leave a job, is it a Swipe? Were you reacting out of discomfort at being asked to take on a new role, your antipathy toward a colleague, or frustration at missing goals? What would happen if you took a step back and reflected on why you felt uncomfortable, disliked a coworker, or were unproductive? If you don't take the time for self-reflection, you're going to Swipe when the going gets tough. You let down your organization, the people who were counting on you, and yourself.

It's MAGIC

Remember the wastewater employee who failed to show up at work for years before anyone noticed? Do you have an employee who retired two years ago and forgot to tell anyone? Or, just maybe, do you disengage from your own work more often than you're willing to admit? You might even feel like Swiping to a new job is inevitable.

Don't give up yet. In 2012 DecisionWise embarked on a three-year project to analyze more than fourteen million employee survey responses in order to understand what created engagement in the workplace. Those three years became a decade-long study with more than fifty million responses that answered the question:

Under what conditions will individuals choose to engage with their work and organization?

The answer is a simple-to-grasp acronym—MAGIC: meaning, autonomy, growth, impact, and connection. When employees find those five elements in an organization—a company, university, hospital, nonprofit, or church—they rarely Swipe. They get things done, finish what they start, endure through discomfort, grow, and advance. MAGIC is the anti-Swipe.

What is MAGIC? We're glad you asked.

- **Meaning** occurs when what is in front of us has purpose beyond the work itself. This is the "why" of our or job. The need for meaning is a fundamentally human one. At some point everyone questions why they're doing what they're doing. If they're unable to find an answer, work becomes mundane. They detach and become disengaged. They Swipe. This is why nine out of ten people are willing to earn less money to do more meaningful work—why the search for meaning is one of the key drivers of the Great Resignation. A study of American workers found they'd be willing to forego 23 percent of their future earnings in order to have a job that was always meaningful.[19] While speaking at a conference, we were discussing how people can find meaning in even the mundane. A woman attending the session raised her hand and told a story. She worked for a medical-staffing company, and this woman spent her workdays placing physicians and other medical personnel in health-care facilities. She admitted she was "simply going through the motions" at this point. It was a good job, but the meaning wasn't there. Then her grandfather fell ill and was placed in an extended care facility. After he passed, the family mentioned how delighted they were with the care he had received. The women realized that the people who so lovingly and professionally cared for her beloved grandfather were the very professionals she had placed in those positions just a few months prior. From that time forward, she was no longer "going through the motions." She was finding health-care professionals who could provide critical care needed by real people—like her grandfather.

- **Autonomy** is the power to shape your environment and work in ways that allow you to perform at your best. Consider this: a movie screenplay is one of the most tightly structured forms of writing. A screenplay must follow a strict form: three acts; "plot points" when the story suddenly changes; a "dark night of the soul," where the main character feels that all is lost; and so on. If you want to have a prayer of having your script produced, you have to follow the rules. Once you've built that framework, however, you, as the screenwriter, have limitless freedom to create an entire world within it. The exterior structure is defined by outside forces that are beyond your control, but within that structure you're in control. That's a terrific analogue for autonomy. Autonomy is about choosing what we do and how we do it, knowing that those choices will lead to the outcome we have in mind, from an award to a promotion. We have control of our fate.

- **Growth** is being stretched and challenged in ways that result in professional progress. It's being better today than we were yesterday. A 2019 research study by LinkedIn found that a quarter of Gen Z and millennials say learning is the number-one thing that makes them happy at work. Over a quarter of Gen Z and millennials say the number-one reason they'd leave their job is because they did not have the opportunity to learn and grow.[20] A 2019 DecisionWise research study backs this up. Lack of opportunity for personal growth is the number-one reason employees leave a company.[21] According to a survey by Glassdoor and Harris Interactive, more applicants—52 percent—wanted to hear about growth opportunities when interviewing for a job than about any other "perk." One-third of employees left a job because of lack of career growth—more than for any other reason.[22] Growth means extending yourself. Getting better. Rising to challenges. Growth also brings novelty and variety. We become bored, distracted, and disengaged when we feel our work is rote, routine, and repetitive. People crave experiences that push their minds and their skills, that are intellectually stimulating, and that offer them the chance to rise to the occasion.

• **Impact** is seeing positive, effective, and worthwhile results from your work. Several years ago, we were asked to speak to a group of 450 health-care professionals about the concept of MAGIC and employee engagement. The organization had come to understand that their level of patient care was dramatically impacted by their level of employee care. The employee experience directly influenced the patient experience. As we were speaking about the level of impact each of them had on hundreds of patients, a nurse supervisor said, "I understand how, as nurses, we have direct impact on our patients. But how does that translate to employees in, say, departments like dietary, transport, or housekeeping? They may not see that level of impact." We saw heads nodding, curious as to what our response might be. There was no need to respond. A woman in the back of the room stood up, grabbing a nearby microphone, and spoke with the fervor of a preacher in a Sunday service. "I work in dietary. My job is to supervise a group of people who are responsible for taking meals to patients three times a day, and sometimes more." Lots of nods and even a few amens. She continued. "None of these patients are at their best when they come to the hospital. While you doctors and nurses are telling them bad news and poking them all day long, my team is bringing them what might be the only joy they experience that day—a good, warm meal. Not only that but every meal is accompanied by a smile and a conversation about them as people, not about their health. That's impact." She sat down. The standing ovation she received from 450 audience members said it all.

- **Connection** is a sense of belonging to something greater than yourself. Through millions of employee surveys, we have found that we can predict whether an individual will stay with an organization by asking them to rate their level of agreement to just one statement:

I feel like I belong here.

Let's look at something seemingly unrelated: obesity. Researchers Nicholas A. Christakis and James H. Fowler discovered that obesity is influenced by a person's social network. Sure. We often surround ourselves with people of similar interests and habits. No surprises there; however, their research showed that even if a twice-removed friend who lives on the other side of the country gains weight you're likely to gain weight too. It sounds crazy and counterintuitive, but the pair has found the same effect in Germany with such phenomena as suicide, politics, and back pain.[23]

Bottom line, we affect and are deeply affected by those around us.

Connection is a basic human need. When we don't feel we are a part of something beyond ourselves, we disengage in the relationship.

Bring the MAGIC

To disengage is to disconnect—from a conversation, a work task, a goal, a relationship, or from simply caring about outcomes and doing the right thing. As we've said, quitting a job isn't necessarily the wrong move. The Great Resignation includes people who have left their positions mindfully and in self-awareness, seeking balance, meaning, community, adventure, or just better pay and some respect. That's great.

Maybe you should leave your job. Maybe you should stick around and reengage. Either way, ask yourself the following questions:

- What would it take to become the best possible version of myself in my current gig?
- How does this job align with what is of greatest worth to me?
- What would the future look like for me in this organization if I were the one to make changes rather than waiting for others to do so?
- Where is MAGIC missing in this organization? Is it possible to find it where I am at currently?
- Is it really missing, or am I just not seeing it?
- What possibilities would I be leaving behind if I walked away?
- What future am I leaving for?
- Am I thinking of leaving out of fear or panic? Am I Swiping?
- If I stop and think about it, is it worth it to stick around for a year to see if MAGIC can make a difference in my experience?
- If I Swipe, what am I Swiping to?

If you're the employer, the questions still apply: Are your people asking those questions? Are you creating an experience in which they can find MAGIC? If you're losing staff hand over fist, the answer is almost certainly no. Go back and read about MAGIC again, and think about what you can do to sprinkle some of it around your organization.

In the end, the goal is to avoid the Swipe, whether you're an employee or the employer. As we've seen with the Great Resignation, Swiping at work creates uncertainty, leaves employers in the lurch, and denies a lot of people what could be a great future. There's nothing wrong with leaving a job or losing an employee, but let's make sure it's for the right reasons.

CHAPTER 5
The Hamster Wheel

Swiping isn't a random event. It follows a predictable cycle—a series of stages that, if we can understand them and see them coming, allow us to interrupt and even prevent the Swipe.

For Patrick Kelly, head of content at book recommendation service Vuibo, the idea of not finishing what we start hit him hard on a personal level. He wrote to us, "I'm a guy that runs roughly ten to fifteen pounds over my 'healthy weight.' I put that in quotes because any physician might place you into some unrealistic weight category where, unless you're Michael Phelps, fat chance of making the cut."

"Yes, four percent body fat is laudable," he continues. "Yet how does that jive with my one-day-a-week pizza or Big Mac splurge? Should I be downright bitter and on-edge with less body fat, or jolly and forward-looking (to that next pepperoni slice) at my current weight? Bottom line, people don't finish what they start, because the end goal isn't all that meaningful. We would all like to look ripped and toned, but the effort to get there is rough. Unless the payoff is something extreme, weight loss especially is a tough thing to accomplish."

California-based artist and writer Niche Brislane shares the same frustrations. "I unfortunately have quite a history of taking on more than I can reasonably do. Tenacity has its downfalls," she writes. "So many of [my failures] have been because I became stretched too thin to get any single thing done. DIY-painted home decor signs. Taking on pet sitting because I wasn't going out of town with new pandemic puppies to worry about. Helping launch a community garden and leaving my own garden projects lacking (after gardening all day for someone else, you hardly want to do it at home too). From the financial pitfalls to disorganization of supplies and lack of storage space to wasted time and money to the sheer panic when one person becomes many, I've seen it all."

As we were writing this book, we surveyed hundreds and interviewed dozens of individuals about their failure to finish the things they started in their lives. We also combed through the millions of points of qualitative and quantitative data from employee surveys. One of the most common shared traits of those interviews and data was the air of powerlessness the participants conveyed regarding their repeated inability to finish things. Over and over, we spoke with smart, driven, educated, successful people who were nevertheless haunted by an inexplicable repeated failure to see even cherished projects and goals through to completion. It would be a stretch to say that those failures had ruined their lives, but they were still left with a resigned sense of "What if?"

This pattern of thinking leads to "blaming and shaming." Some blame the external situation, abdicating ownership and handing it over to the environment or the organization. It's easy to blame the perceived bad work setting on the employer rather than on oneself. It may be more convenient to blame the other party for a relationship turned sour than it is to look in the mirror.

It's also easy to swing to the other end of the spectrum, berating oneself in a downward spiral of despair and self-pity. On one hand, people with a habit of starting things but not finishing them sometimes embark on a lifelong campaign of bitter self-accusation, tearing themselves apart over their failures to stay on task and get things done, often convincing themselves that they are the only people to fall into this maddening pattern. On the other, the same folks are convinced there's a class of "successful" individuals out in the world—with names like Musk, Branson, Winfrey, and Bezos— who somehow complete everything they begin, aren't wracked with self-doubt, and never engage in procrastination. Compared to those mythical titans, these average Joes (and Janes) are convinced they should feel ashamed of themselves, and so they do.

As we've said, there is a sizable body of academic work around procrastination, a form of self-sabotage that bears similarities to the Swipe. Much of this research not only supports the idea that procrastination and not finishing what we set out to finish are negative phenomena but that they come with a heavy weight of guilt, shame, and anxiety.

Psychologist Dr. Tim Pychyl tested this by giving forty-five college students a pager—this was the mid-1990s, when pagers were still a thing—and tracking them for five days leading up to an important school deadline. Eight times a day, he paged the students, who reported how much they were procrastinating as well as their emotional state. The more difficult the preparation for the deadline became, the more likely the students were to put off preparation in favor of doing something enjoyable. As they did this, however, they also reported higher levels of guilt. Pychyl concluded that while procrastinators feel a compulsion toward enjoyable engagements that distract from the task before them, the dread they experience at having the task still hanging over their heads causes emotional distress. They recognize, as he wrote, that they are causing themselves "temporal harm."[1]

So not finishing what we start isn't a benign phenomenon; it's also not an ephemeral one. There are predictable psychological wheels turning when people Swipe. What feels like the inexplicable caprice of undisciplined minds is actually a fairly ordinary mechanism at work: our brains pivoting us away from likely pain and fear and simultaneously seeking pleasure and comfort. We're wired to do this, and as Ruhul Kader, cofounder and CEO of Future Startup and author of *Rethinking Failure: A Short Guide to Living an Entrepreneurial Life*, writes, our mental tool kit is filled with tricks that grease the wheels for us to procrastinate or quit while dodging guilt or shame: "Four enemies of finishing are distractions, addictions, fear, and lethargy. These play a critical role in taking us off the path. The source of all these enemies appears to be the same. When faced with a difficult task, our general response is taking resort to distraction. You may ask, why so? Because it is easier and comfortable. We are always seeking comfort."[2]

The Hamster Wheel

As is turns out, the Swipe follows a predicable series of steps closely related to that natural impulse to flee from discomfort and run toward pleasure. That means, among other things, we can exercise some control over this seemingly reflexive reaction that causes us to abandon once-cherished goals. But before we examine the mechanisms that allow us to catch ourselves in our moments of discomfort and avoid Swiping, let's take a look at the behavioral stages that lead us to that critical crossroads.

Swiping behavior tends to be cyclical, so our visual representation of that behavior is cyclical as well, looking like a wheel. In fact, because so many people Swipe habitually, unable to escape the endless "try-quit-try-quit-try" cycle, we've labeled the cycle the Hamster Wheel. Like a pet rodent in a cage scurrying on an exercise wheel and getting nowhere, we often scramble around our own wheel, trying and failing over and over again, never understanding why we don't achieve what we set out to do, or why we can't seem to find happiness.

Time to understand and change things. First off, this is the Hamster Wheel:

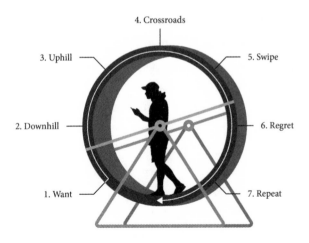

The Want

On the lower left corner of the wheel, we find the Want, the thing you set out to achieve. But there are really two kinds of goal setting that relate to the Swipe. The first we call *Strong Wants*. A Strong Want involves an affirmative plan of action designed to produce a precise goal: losing twenty pounds, advancing my career, writing one thousand words a day, that sort of thing. Research shows that setting such goals leads to higher levels of motivation, self-esteem, self-confidence, and autonomy,[3] and additional research has shown that setting Strong Goals increases the chances of success.[4]

Strong Wants bear a compelling link to positive psychology, in which an optimistic mindset and an orientation on solutions, not problems, leads goal seekers to commit to specific actions, set realistic goals, and build stronger self-efficacy. One of the hallmarks of working with Strong Wants is that people setting them learn as much as possible about the path they're about to attempt so they're more prepared for the inevitable hard work and bumps in the road.

Unfortunately, people who Swipe tend not to have Strong Wants, but *Weak Wants*, making it more difficult to engage. Weak Wants are wishy-washy and indistinct, expressed in language like, "I'd really like to," or "Maybe I should try that." They might be New Year's resolutions casually contemplated on January 1, ideas for home design caught on Pinterest, or dares from a friend, nothing more. Instead of definitive plans, actions, and time lines, there's a vague sense of wanting to try something, but little more than that. That flies in the face of everything psychology teaches about successfully setting and reaching goals, embodied in the work of American psychologist Edwin Locke, who argued that for goals to lead to desired outcomes, they should:

- be clear and specific,
- be challenging but attainable,
- come with feedback,
- be used to evaluate the person's performance,
- come with deadlines, and
- be focused more on learning than on performance.[5]

Because Weak Wants come with none of these safety mechanisms—because they're often casual, poorly planned, vague, or high-impossible goals, known as "stretch goals"—they're subject to what we call the cost theory of goal attainment. Simply put, the higher the "cost" of a goal, from the time and money invested in planning and pursuing it to the social impact of quitting, the more likely the person pursuing the goal is to persist in trying to reach it. Weak Wants come with few, if any, consequences for quitting, other than personal regret or frustration, so the cost of giving up is minimal.

Weak Wants are Swipe Wants. This is where the cycle starts. A man decides blithely to train to run his first marathon in three months, unaware that's a woefully inadequate amount of time and ignorant of what such training requires. Or a woman is directed to learn her company's new customer relationship management software suite so she can train her peers on it. But she doesn't make a plan or do advance research, so she jumps in blindly. From here, the wheel lurches into motion with little or no preparation, support, or reality checks to keep it moving.

The Downhill

Once we set our Weak Want, we begin taking action, and that leads to the Downhill. This is the beginning stage, where words come easily to the fledgling novelist and where the would-be marathoner believes that because running one mile was doable, maybe running 26.2 miles won't be so bad either. We referred to this earlier as *page-one energy.* Like the cyclist flying down a long downhill grade, everything is effortless and pleasurable.

But the real trouble with the Downhill segment of our wheel isn't that the work feels giddily simple. It's that this segment burdens us with painfully unrealistic expectations of what's to come. In setting Weak Wants, we don't learn about the demands we're likely to face in achieving them—trudging through page three hundred of a fiction manuscript or dealing with the pain that comes with trying to run fifteen miles—or what it will take to meet them. We're completely unprepared when things become difficult. We delude ourselves that "It will always be this way."

Because the Downhill is so enjoyable, there's a theory that it can even become addictive to start and then quickly abandon projects and goals just to enjoy the effortless early stages. This makes sense, as our brains are designed to seek out pleasurable sensations. And if getting those hits of dopamine through months of sweat and toil is asking too much, we'll get them from a week or two of improbable tailwinds before reality comes crashing down on us.

NERD ALERT!

Being on the Downhill, momentum-positive part of the Hamster Wheel can feel a great deal like being in the state of flow, which the late psychologist Mihály Csíkszentmihályi described as a state of complete immersion in an activity, where one action flows naturally into another, the mind is completely focused, and results seem to come effortlessly. This is also called being "in the zone." When we're on the Downhill, however, what we experience is a "false flow," because we're at the early stages of the task, when the challenges are not yet very great, and few, if any, obstacles have reared their ugly heads to give us pause about our ability to reach our goals.

This state is also known as *optimism bias*, when a person's expectation is vastly better than the outcome that follows. As psychologist Tali Sharot writes, "Humans . . . exhibit a pervasive and surprising bias: when it comes to predicting what will happen to us tomorrow, next week, or fifty years from now, we overestimate the likelihood of positive events, and underestimate the likelihood of negative events."[6]

This bias, or the ability to fool ourselves into believing that completing a task will always be as easy as it is during those first trouble-free days, can serve a useful purpose. By presuming that good outcomes and positive life events are more likely, and negative outcomes and events unlikely or even impossible, we remain hopeful. We strive, sometimes foolishly, for the ridiculous and improbable, and in doing so occasionally accomplish so-called "moon shots" that we would never otherwise have dared. A pinch of healthy self-delusion can be a good thing.

But when we have no plan, when we've learned nothing about the road ahead, when we're overconfident in our own abilities because we believe irrationally that that road will always have a downhill pitch, things go sideways. Eventually, we reach the bottom of the hill.

The Uphill

The third stage of the wheel is as predictable as the first, but briefer. Imagine you're kayaking a waterway. At first you're traveling with the current, and the wind is at your back. Paddling is easy and enjoyable, and you have time to look around and appreciate the sights onshore. Then the current changes. The wind shifts until it's blowing directly in your face. Suddenly paddling goes from being easy, nearly without effort, to strenuous, tedious, and exhausting. Sweating and panting from the exertion, you can scarcely believe that just a short while ago you were scoffing at the people who warned you this trip would test your endurance. Now you believe them.

Now you're appalled and even angry that your experience has gone from being deceptively easy to being brutally difficult.

The Uphill represents the point in the early stages of a new goal attempt when giddy, naive ease gives way to grunting, straining drudgery. It's when your inner voice says, *Oh, crap, this will be a lot more work than I thought.* The real world—in which nothing of value comes easily, and excellence requires years of experience and repetitive practice—intrudes on the delusional aura of the Weak Want and reveals the goal setter's commitment to be shockingly fragile and lacking in self-awareness or preparation.

This is the fifty-page point in that new novel. It's the plateau in your fitness program, where you realize you've been working out every day for a month, and the scale hasn't budged. It's the six-month mark in the new job, where you're out of training and have to make an unpopular decision. It's the three-month place in a relationship, where the romantic infatuation has finally faded, and you say to yourself, *Wait a sec, not everything he does is adorable. This is going to take work.*

The transition point from the Downhill to the Uphill—known as the *vertex*—is also the psychological transition point for someone attempting something new or difficult without *a priori* awareness of the potential pitfalls and quagmires involved. When the vertex is reached, one of two psychological processes typically begins to play out:

1. If you educated yourself about the difficulty of the task you were undertaking and the likely sticking points you would reach along the way to your goal, hitting the vertex is accompanied by recognition, along with a sense of resolve. You did your homework, so you knew this was coming. You talked to people who had run marathons, so you knew that between mile six and mile seven you were likely to feel deep fatigue and a stitch in your side. You're not surprised; however, you are ready to keep pushing through the hard part, and you have strategies to help you do so.

2. If you jumped into the task with zero preparation and a cup that runneth over with unearned self-confidence, you're not only stunned by the abrupt change of fortune but you're offended. You feel betrayed and embarrassed—and possibly an unpleasant foreshadowing of failure in the pit of your stomach. The microscopic beginnings of a rationalization for quitting might be taking shape in your unconscious.

The first person is unlikely to Swipe. The second person is nearly certain to, not because they lack the ability to finish what they started but because their emotional reaction to the vertex leaves them stunned and resentful. How *dare* reality lacerate the false sense of superiority they've been enjoying! This mentality is related to what has become popularly known as the Dunning-Kruger effect. This bias, described by social psychologists David Dunning and Justin Kruger, suggests that some individuals are comically over-confident because they are in fact too incompetent to perceive their own incompetence.[7] A related phenomenon applies to the Swipe.

Instead, transition to the Uphill shatters that delusion of competence and leaves the individual not only feeling discouraged and overwhelmed at how unfit or unprepared they are but feeling stupid and unworthy for deceiving themselves into believing the goal would be easy to attain. The person hasn't Swiped—yet—but is nevertheless already laying a groundwork of rationalizations to explain why they should.

An extreme example of this dynamic at work is the bizarre story of sailor Donald Crowhurst. Crowhurst, an erratic, quixotic English entrepreneur and self-promoter, bet his wealth and reputation on building a boat and competing in the 1968 *Sunday Times* Golden Globe Race, an around-the-world, single-handed, nonstop sailboat race that attracted the most experienced, daring sailors in the world. Crowhurst, who had no experience sailing the extremely dangerous waters of the Southern Ocean around Antarctica, nevertheless feigned confidence and spent everything he had to build his boat, the *Teignmouth Electron*, and in October 1968 departed from England to begin the race south.

It quickly became apparent that Crowhurst's marine engineering skills were no better than his sailing skills. The *Teignmouth Electron* was unseaworthy, and trying to navigate it through the ferocious storms and massive waves of the Southern Ocean would have been suicide. But Crowhurst also knew that quitting the race would have meant disgrace and financial ruin, so he spent weeks gusting back and forth in a lightly trafficked area of the South Atlantic, falsifying his written log and radio broadcasts to give the impression he was circumnavigating—an easy thing to do in the days before satellite tracking and radio beacons.

Logs and audio recordings found on the *Teignmouth Electron* later show that over the weeks that he secretly cruised around isolated areas of the ocean Crowhurst's thinking became disordered and deeply delusional, and eventually he slipped into a state of psychosis. When the race concluded, and searchers finally located the empty boat drifting and undamaged, without its sole occupant, they concluded that a despondent and psychologically broken Crowhurst jumped into the Atlantic and committed suicide—perhaps the ultimate example of the Swipe from someone whose identity had been shattered.[8]

Crossroads

> *Two roads diverged in a yellow wood,*
> *And sorry I could not travel both*
> *And be one traveler, long I stood*
> *And looked down one as far as I could*
> *To where it bent in the undergrowth.*
>
> —"The Road Not Taken," Robert Frost

Eventually, as the Uphill drags on and on, and drudgery turns to discouragement and exhaustion, we reach the Crossroads. This is Frost's "road not taken." But the mental process of choosing which branching path to follow into the forest is not the carefully considered, mildly rueful process of Frost's protagonist, who deliberately elects to walk down the less traveled pathway and cannot help a pang of regret that he will never see what was down the path he chose not to follow. The cognitive circuitry of the Swipe is different.

The Crossroads is the point on the Hamster Wheel where we face a decision: continue chasing the Want that's become so arduous, or abandon it. This is where preparation, education, realistic expectations, and self-efficacy help certain individuals stay the course, while others who might have blundered blindly into their attempt out of ego or naivete simply give up. This is the inflection point of the Swipe.

At the Crossroads, self-awareness and intentionality play a pivotal role. Consider that at this point the aspiring marathoner or would-be Hollywood screenwriter might be struggling after weeks or months of frustration and futility. The intoxication of the new is long gone, and it's clear that what lies ahead is more struggle, self-doubt, and pain. In his bestselling book *A Walk in the Woods*, Bill Bryson hits on this when he discusses his apprehension at the idea of returning to the Appalachian Trail full time after months of day hiking: "This time . . . there was no small, endearingly innocent pulse of excitement, that keen and eager frisson that comes with venturing into the unknown with gleaming, untried equipment. This time I knew exactly what was out there—a lot of long, taxing miles, steep rocky mountains, hard shelter floors, hot days without showers, unsatisfying meals cooked on a temperamental stove."[9]

But someone with a high degree of metacognition, aware of the Swipe and their own reflex to avoid discomfort, can have a different experience at the Crossroads. If we're educated about what the pursuit of our goal might bring, and aware of our own thoughts, we can stand at the junction of the two choices and make a conscious decision to lean into difficulty and remain engaged with our goal.

Alternatively, we can choose to "tap out." But in this case, we're not disengaging. There's no panicked pulling of the rip cord.

HOW NOT TO SWIPE

When you have invested time, expense, and effort to try something grand, only to find that you're nowhere close to your goal, the effect on morale and motivation can be crippling. The solution: Don't allow expectations to accrue only to be dashed the first time you get a reality check. Create your own intentional reality checks. When pursuing a rigorous goal, lift your nose off the grindstone once in a while to do a check on where you really are with regard to your goal. Doing this can puncture the euphoria of believing you're much farther along than you are, but if that belief is a lie, what good is it? Better to get a true assessment of how you're progressing because doing so will prevent explosions that sap the will to go on.

The Swipe

Look at the graphic of the Hamster Wheel. Identify the point where the Swipe occurs. You can see that the act of Swiping causes the individual to bypass all the later points on the circle that have to do with reflection: *consideration*, *identity*, *values*, *ego*, *entitlement*, and *self-worth*. Essentially, the act of Swiping neutralizes the brain's executive functions—the dimensions of our cognition that compare, contrast, and speculate on alternate possible outcomes and prescribe courses of action to help us overcome our shortcomings. With the

Swipe, those extraordinary abilities lay on a different highway and might as well be in another country with closed borders.

When we Swipe, we dash down the fork in the road that leads away from our difficult pursuit. Initially, the overwhelming feeling is one of relief. No more pain or anticipation of pain; no more feeling inadequate or untalented. With the fear of failure—of being exposed as a fraud—vanquished, thoughts like, *Thank goodness that's behind me. What was I thinking?* rush through the mind.

But there's another interesting effect that occurs when someone Swipes, and it might be the most telling of all. Upon Swiping, the individual rejects the chance to take an off-ramp toward the Real and elects to remain in the territory of the Illusory. The person casually training for a marathon without the slightest idea what they're doing is stuck in an illusion, and upon accepting that what they're trying to do is impossible they choose not to reflect on their experience and grapple with why they failed. Instead, they sprint past uncomfortable questions like a superstitious child running past a creepy-looking house, covering their eyes for fear of what they might see.

Because of this, Swiping is a one-way ticket. The individual chooses not to engage in any candid analysis of why they failed, what learning or preparation might be in order for another attempt—or even if they should be making the attempt at all. There's no path back to where they diverged because there's no accounting, no confrontation with the fears, self-doubts, psychological triggers, or issues of pride or identity that might have led them astray. In the initial stages of the Swipe, ignorance is indeed bliss.

Regret

Until . . .

When the adrenaline rush of escape fades, we're left with acute, sometimes overwhelming regret. Regret is the act of blaming oneself for a bad outcome, but accepted wisdom suggests persuasively that we tend to harbor sharper pangs of regret for the things we don't do rather than the things we attempt and fail. This is regret elevated to a blistering guilty verdict against our character. If we saw something through and failed at it, at least we can still bolster our self-esteem with the thought that we gave it our best and pushed to the end. But giving up in a reactive panic of self-doubt? There's no salvation in that in the mind of someone who has Swiped. Only shame and cowardice.

Writer William Barton said of regret, "Regret, they say, is the most expensive thing in the world, but it's a lie. Regret is free; you get to have as much regret as you want. And then, when you're done wanting regret, you find it's yours to keep forever."[10] He had it right—regret has a long half-life, and not just because we feel remorse over squandered opportunities and adventures that we never had. Regret is corrosive because it seems to confirm that our darkest doubts about ourselves are correct. We believed we would fall short or chicken out at something we've aspired to try for years, and then we verify that belief by walking away as soon as things get tough. This is the "I'm a loser" moment that inevitably comes calling once the exultation fades. That severe judgment stays with us, sometimes for life.

But the truly insidious part of the Regret stage is that it compels us to try to exterminate it. Regret is so powerful that it can make us forget how much we've suffered and rush back to assuage it by repeating the same doomed effort. Why do so many people attempt their first novel twenty times without success, or keep dating the same kind of person over and over? They are trying to erase the mental stink of failure and the verdict it imposes on them.

The terrible reality is, without self-awareness and the ability to see the Swipe coming, most people who fall into this pattern of regret, remorse, repeat will continue to leap in blindly, unprepared, and doom themselves to an endless cycle of heartache.

Repeat

Driven by overpowering shame and regret, at this stage we really are on a hamster wheel, running hard and getting nowhere. Compelled to wash the taste of surrender from our mouths, sooner or later we end up back here, at the beginning, ready to embark on the same fruitless course of actions leading once again to giving up.

Without the deep awareness born of painful self-scrutiny and rough experience, we follow our emotions blindly, convincing ourselves, *This time will be different*, when it will likely be anything but.

The Hamster Wheel is a closed system. It's difficult to escape without radically changing how we perceive our own identity and thoughts, our sense of self-esteem and self-efficacy, and the challenges that lay between our aspiration and the achievement of our goal. But undertaken they can be, and we will talk about how. There is another version of the wheel, one you can access when you don't Swipe, the one based in reflection, self-awareness, and acceptance of reality.

We'll get to that other wheel in chapter 10. But first, let's dig deeper into the mechanics of the Swipe.

CHAPTER 6

There's an App for That

> The addictive, seductive power of the smartphone has changed how we think about reality, even unconsciously. Because smart devices make it so easy to swipe a screen and change our situation, we've become conditioned to be impatient with discomfort or dissatisfaction and more likely to flee from something that doesn't work for us in the moment for something new.

If we want to conquer the Swipe, we need to know why we Swipe, and the best place to start that search is with the technology that inspired the term. Ironically, we begin with a device that aims to help us be *more* engaged, not less.

The Light Phone II is a smartphone, at least in name. With it, you can make and receive calls, send text messages, and listen to podcasts. But you can't check your email, take pictures, or—and this is critical—surf social media. Why would anyone want such a barbaric device? Among other reasons, to reduce anxiety and depression, which research has shown are higher in people with so-called "smartphone dependency."

But the real genius of the Light Phone II and similarly limited devices is that they minimize the smartphone's ability to distract us from being in the moment, from experiencing our lives as they happen. Before the smartphone existed, mobile phones like the Motorola Razr could make calls and receive primitive text messages, period. Then along came devices like the PalmPilot and BlackBerry, with their ability to pull email out of the ether. Suddenly millions of businesspeople, Wall Street traders, and Hollywood worker bees were addicted to their "Crackberries." The mobile phone had gone from being a communication tool to something that changed how we interacted with the world—and each other. With the debut of the iPhone in 2007, the evolution accelerated.

That technology, particularly the smartphone, has altered our behavior seems inarguable. For example, in a 2017 study, a team led by Adrian Ward, a professor at The University of Texas at Austin, conducted a study comparing the scores on cognitive tests between people who had phones on their desks and those who left their phones elsewhere. Even with the phones powered down, the participants with phones scored lower.[1] "Our phones represent something that is almost always, at least hypothetically, more rewarding than what's going on in front of us," Ward said.[2]

It's hard to imagine a more perfect description of the psychological cueing that leads to the Swipe.

Technology Is Changing Us

In 2013, the UN released findings that were both interesting and disturbing. According to the report, at that time, of Earth's 7 billion inhabitants, 6 billion had access to a cell phone. Not surprising? Perhaps, until you learn that only 4.5 billion had proper sanitation. Is that right? Roughly 1.5 billion people had cell phones but no toilet or sanitary waste disposal?[3]

Again and again, scientists have found that for billions of people smartphones have become surrogate worlds, alternate realities that we prefer to the chaotic, stubbornly rigid world of obstreperous coworkers, nagging partners, late buses, and rotten service. In fact, anthropologists have found that smartphone users commonly regard their handsets with the same warmth and sense of safety and intimacy as they do their *homes.*

In early 2021, anthropologists from University College London published the results of a year in the field spent documenting people's smartphone habits in nine countries.[4] They found that for many their smartphones have become "where they live" psychically and emotionally. Their phones are where they maintain relationships, connect with family or colleagues to solve problems, and learn what's happening in the lives of other people, even from halfway across the world. "The smartphone is no longer just a device that we use, it's become the place where we live," said researcher Daniel Miller. "The flip side of that for human relationships is that at any point, whether over a meal, a meeting or other shared activity, a person we're with can just disappear, having 'gone home' to their smartphone."[5]

Miller and his colleagues have compared this ability to mentally "go home" to the teenager's bedroom with a "Do Not Enter" sign on the door and called it "the death of proximity." They assert that it's changed our society by forcing us to accept that even when we are physically in the same space we can now be utterly alone, as reflected perfectly in that 2014 *National Geographic* photo contest grand prize–winning photo we referenced earlier. By giving us a frictionless, seductive means to instantly alter our perceptions not just of time and place but experience, we have made it easy to disappear from distressing circumstances that, if we simply leaned into them and saw them through to their conclusions, could prove rewarding, even transformative.

Scott Ferguson, founder of golf product review site iovergolf.com, understands this. "Every day I look for new things to do," he told us in an email interview. "I explore a lot of hobbies and pastimes, and the reason for them is I want to grow. However, I don't often continue or pursue them long term for one reason. I fear failure. To be honest, I'm not gonna admit that I am a perfectionist. Because in my eyes, I'm not. There are days I give my all, and there are days I give nothing at all. So I'm not a perfectionist. I just don't want to fail at things I want to be good at."

"But what I've learned with this mindset is that thinking that I'll fail is what's gonna make me fail," he continues. "Because it stops me at the beginning. Because it halts me in my process. I didn't fail because I'm not good at it. I failed because I didn't try further. Ever since I realized that, I just did everything. I continued pursuing the things I started. It's hard and demotivating in the beginning, but it's the process that's promising, not the ending. It's the process that's making me grow, not the results."

Technology is not the only force that's made us apt to Swipe away from the processes that make us uncomfortable but help us grow, but it's the most visible. And since we know that continual exposure to that tech has changed not only how we behave but how our brains function, let's take a closer look at why smart devices have gained so much power over us and had such a profound impact on our ability to engage in and finish what we start.

The Tinder Effect

When we talk about the swipe gesture, the first thing that comes to mind for many is the dating app. Launched in 2012, Tinder quickly made "swiping right" into a meme and cultural shorthand for saying, "Yes, I'd love to," to an amorous advance. But few people appreciate just how much Tinder and its app cousins altered how we perceive the world.

If you spent any time in the online dating world, you know what it was like pre-Tinder. If you didn't, let us tell you a story. Once upon a time, long after you actually met people from school or down at the club, there were online dating sites like Match.com, Matchmaker, OkCupid, and Plenty of Fish, and they all followed the same basic operational template. You would open an account, create a profile, list the search filters for the type of person you wanted to meet, and then scroll through profile after profile of people who fit your parameters for age, race, height, body type, interests, etc. It was a lot like scanning a page from your high school yearbook looking for someone cute.

The trouble with those previous online dating services was that interest only had to be monodirectional for one member to reach out to another. If you thought someone was attractive, you could email him or her. As a result, women tended to be buried in emails from guys, only a small percentage of whom they might find even remotely interesting. But Tinder's structure changed the game. Now, instead of scanning profile after profile, you scrolled to one new photo, and then the next, quickly swiping left if you didn't find the person attractive but swiping your finger right across the screen if you thought the person was good-looking. More important, the person whose picture you swiped would be alerted that you had found them attractive, and only if the feeling was mutual would you be allowed to communicate on the platform.

This seismic shift in "techno courtship" had several important effects. First, it quickly became addictive. Being told that someone finds you attractive delivers that same tiny squirt of dopamine to the brain's pleasure circuitry as sex or chocolate, so the more Tinder users swiped, the more they wanted to swipe—not to mention the anticipatory power of believing that your soul mate might be right around the next virtual corner kept people hooked.

But even more relevant for our conversation was the instant gratification Tinder enabled, and the way it empowered us to instantly kick unattractive potential suitors to the curb without a second thought. In the old days of reading profiles, you might have to spend at least a few minutes learning about someone before brooming them because of their unhealthy preoccupation with Precious Moments figurines or the fact that they still lived with Mom. A study[6] by Princeton psychologist Alex Todorov shows that we perceive attractiveness within one-tenth of a second. On Tinder, you spend barely any time deciding if someone is "hot or not," and if not, you react by swiping left.

The Tinder Effect is an expectation so many of us have internalized: Not only *can* we assess our circumstances in an eyeblink, and then instantly abandon those circumstances for something potentially better, but we are *entitled* to do so! No reflection on ourselves or the situation is required. In fact, reflection and analysis are frowned upon. Why waste the time when we can just Swipe our way into new potential?

This belief has been boosted into popular consciousness by technologies like *augmented reality* and *virtual reality*. Augmented reality applications on smartphones allow us to view the world through a visual informational overlay showing, for example, the restaurants on a given city block along with their menus and recent reviews. Virtual reality has been around for years in a crude form, but that's changing. State-of-the-art VR systems, like Oculus Rift, make it possible for users to disappear into fully immersive worlds with sensory feedback and interactivity. The reality of these environments is so convincing that psychotherapists are even using them for "exposure therapy," treating patients for debilitating phobias.

In other words, intentional or otherwise, technology has created an unconscious expectation in a substantial fraction of the population that life is *reality optional*. If we are unhappy or discomfited by the present, we can disengage with the push of a button, the launch of a new app, or the swipe of a glass screen. Even if we don't consciously believe that changing a VR environment will bring about permanent transformation in our "real" lives, the impulse is there, and it's the impulse that matters here. It's the impulse that leads us to quit before we finish what we've begun.

You might not think you're affected by this, but you are. Here's a simple but revealing way to prove it. When you're writing something but not using a computer—writing a list by hand on a yellow legal pad, for instance, or a birthday card—how often do you make a mistake and then find yourself looking for the undo function, just for a second? Technology has *conditioned* you. We're all being conditioned to *feel*, just for an instant, that the reality of atoms and molecules is as malleable as that of bits and bytes.

NERD ALERT!

The concept of swiping right or left on Tinder was inspired by a famous experiment conducted in the 1940s by American psychologist B. F. Skinner. Skinner conditioned hungry pigeons to believe that food randomly delivered into a tray was prompted by pecking, essentially turning pecking for food into a game. If a pigeon took a random action just before receiving food, such as knocking its head against the cage wall, it would repeat that action irrationally, even superstitiously, on the off chance that the food would come again. On Tinder, the same reward mechanism applies. Users swipe obsessively across profiles, spending an average of ninety minutes a day on the app, because the anticipation that the next swipe, or the next one, or the next one, will produce someone hot and datable.

The End of Ambiguity

That conditioning matters. When we Swipe, we're reacting as though the physical world can be "switched to a friendlier channel" in the same way the digital world can. When we experience momentary panic, terror, or doubt, that conditioning makes us reflexively sprint away from something we perceive as dangerous to our self-image or emotional equanimity. This *reality overlay* seduces us into cutting and running from the difficult work of self-evolution.

The changes wrought by the ubiquity and computing muscle of smartphones are not limited to the effects detailed by Nicholas Carr in his infamous 2017 *Wall Street Journal* piece "How Smartphones Hijack Our Minds."[7] In that article, Carr argued—correctly, in our view—that there's an inverse correlation between our use of smartphones and the agility and power of the human intellect. One example of this intellectual atrophy is the decay of our ability to remember phone numbers. Once upon a time, we all had a catalog of home and work numbers in our heads because we had no other way to store them. Now we just go to our contacts app or order Siri to call the office.

Still, such self-imposed cognitive effects are relatively small potatoes. Most of the time, they don't interfere with our ability to function or to thrive in our daily lives. But we can't say the same about the effects of the reality overlay that leads us to Swipe. One of the most pernicious of these is what we call the *ambiguity deficit*.

Remember back when navigating the highways and byways on a road trip meant pulling a AAA map out of your glove compartment, unfolding it (we won't even start on the refolding nightmare), and using your index finger to find the optimal route to your destination? Now, except for those rare instances when you're in a location too remote for cellular service, you probably use a smartphone GPS app. Back in ancient times, we used books to look up information—encyclopedias, dictionaries, newspaper archives on microfilm, and so on. Now we use Google—or we did. Even searching via Google demanded that we use our faculties to gauge the reliability of both the results we found and their sources. But today, more and more often, we rely on Alexa or Siri to retrieve information for us. We've outsourced our perspicacity.

Don't get us wrong—we're writers and researchers. We're grateful that a universe of facts and historical accounts are at our fingertips. It's incredible. The availability of tools like Google has made us all more productive. But technology has imposed costs on how we interface with the world, and one of those costs is a growing inability to cope with and appreciate ambiguity. In the analog past, information was not bidirectional. We had to seek it out; it didn't come to us at the drop of a hyperlink or a verbal command to a smart speaker. Because of this, our efforts to glean knowledge—the best route to a city, info on how to rewire an electrical junction box, job openings, historical data on our family tree—were always marginally successful. We rarely found all the information that was out there, never saw the complete picture. So we had to surmise, fill in the gaps, and make intuitive leaps in order to move forward. We became comfortable taking action without knowing everything in advance. We were cool with some uncertainly because we had to be. We didn't need to have a full picture or all the answers in order to engage.

Now we have tremendously valuable tools like Siri, Google Maps, Glassdoor, and Ancestry.com. The list goes on and on and on. Thanks to Amazon, flipping through the offerings at a cool used-record store, hoping to stumble upon something amazing, has been replaced by the search field. In fact, we don't even need to search—algorithms do the work for us, serving up related options through multiple open browser tabs based on previous searches and what's already in our online collection. Treasure hunting, with its wonderful, laughable surprises, is dying. We have become apprehensive, even fearful, about taking a step if our data is murky or if we don't have turn-by-turn directions—even if those directions lead us to drive into a marina or off a bridge, both of which happen with disturbing frequency.

Technology has been hard at work banishing ambiguity from our lives—or, more to the point, it's been scrubbing life of the *appearance* of ambiguity. There's still plenty of ambiguity for us to navigate in our relationships, our jobs, our health, our ideas about meaning and purpose. But search algorithms and titanic databases have fostered the falsely comforting notion that concrete data and surety are available about everything, and we really want that to be true. Resolve your parental abandonment issues? There must be an app for that, right? Expecting mathematically precise solutions to everything, we're losing our power to cope with situations that are messy, like love, death, and morality. Looking for a relationship? We *know* there are apps for that.

But the ambiguity deficit isn't just about our ability to process. We're also losing our appreciation of uncertainty, of mystery. In the past, our delight in road trips, research projects, and forays into back-alley shop stalls came from not knowing what we would find. We might duck into a hole-in-the-wall café and find a hidden gem or end up with salmonella poisoning. Not knowing made the experience more piquant and exciting, and it made discovering true gems all the more delightful. Now we have Yelp and TripAdvisor. We're to the point where if we don't know what's to come and can't rely on fifty-plus reviews of at least four-and-a-half stars, we can't even take the first step into something new.

It's not hard to imagine how falling out of love with ambiguity makes it easier to quit what we've started. By definition, you don't know what to expect when you start something new. You're on the road not taken, and plan though you might, your foresight is always limited. Now, thanks to technology that purports to give us all the answers, we're more likely to feel trepidation than thrill when we can't see around the next bend in the road. It's all too easy to pull over, abandon the vehicle, and walk away rather than savor the risk and exhilaration of the unknown.

HOW NOT TO SWIPE

Stop depending on your smartphone to gather intel about the people, places, and experiences laid out before you from day to day. Stop scouring restaurant reviews before choosing a place for lunch. Quit learning everything you can about an ancient district of a city like Paris or Rome before you even board the plane. When driving from point A to point B in unfamiliar territory, trust your instincts and road smarts to guide you, and if you're worried about getting lost, use a paper map, not Google Maps. Get in the habit of not having foreknowledge, of being cool with uncertainty. We're not suggesting that you not use your smart device to do things like book the best airfare or remotely deposit checks; activities that save you money or increase efficiency are always worthwhile. But back away from the erroneous belief that you need to know every detail about the world around you to avoid catastrophe. A dicey meal at an unfamiliar dive can be an adventure, not a hardship. Getting pleasantly lost walking the streets of Venice or New Orleans can lead to magical discoveries. Break yourself of the habit of curation, and you'll be more apt to embrace the imprecision of your own aspirations and not Swipe.

Programmed Helplessness

From this perspective, is it fair to assert that smart technology, in granting us the illusion of near-absolute control over one dimension of our reality, has actually diminished our control over ourselves? We think it is. Millions upon millions of us now live in tightly controlled simulacra of reality governed by the activity of apps; access to big data; and the unending flow of connectivity through servers, wireless routers, and cellular towers. Millions more aspire to do so.

Social pundits claim that the easy availability of technology has turned each of us into potential full-time curators of our lives. But the literal definition of *curation* is "the action or process of selecting, organizing, and looking after the items in a collection or exhibition," and while that may apply to those who carefully stage every waking moment of their lives as public artifacts to be shared on social media, the dimension of the Swipe is something more.

In our view, the role of humans in this society has become that of an interface between the messy, imprecise real world and the intelligence-gathering powers of our phones. In essence, we've become *field operatives* collecting intel designed to mitigate the natural uncertainty of life and replace it with preordained comfort and success. As the prevalence of Swiping shows, this obsession with smoothing out the rough spots in life's journey can come with more detriments than benefits.

If we refuse to stick a toe out the front door of our homes without precurating every possible experience with reviews, guidebook write-ups, and maps, then sure, we'll probably have more friction-less experiences. We can reject anything that risks not coming up to our standards or that's too unfamiliar, not ever giving ourselves time to fully engage in what's before us. But friction creates heat and light. Without the reversals and surprises life can throw at us, our self-efficacy never blossoms. We lose out on experiences that make us stronger, that teach us and expand our worldview, that delight us in ways we couldn't have anticipated.

We're not suggesting we shouldn't use the technological tools at our disposal to minimize misery and inconvenience in our lives. That would be ridiculous; however, our ability to adapt to circumstances and lean into discomfort would be sharpened to a keener edge if we stopped trying to pave over all the bumps and potholes of daily life by using our tech as a sort of low-grade precognition. Consider the effect this might have on the five elements of our MAGIC—our meaning, autonomy, growth, impact, and connection. Experiencing the organic ups and downs of living would help more of us believe in our own resilience and ability to get things done, and that would reduce the number of Swipes away from cherished goals.

Entitled to the Downhill Ride

But the most important impact technology has on the Swipe might also be the most insidious. In making it easier and faster to communicate, in serving as our alarm clock and calendar, in reducing friction in everything from retail to banking to employment to dating, smart technology has made daily life less troublesome and more efficient. There's no question that it's enhanced our productivity, and in the era of worldwide remote work it's also given millions more professional freedom than they ever thought possible.

The trouble comes when our brains—always searching for the easiest glide path to get what we want in order to dodge complication and conserve energy—misapprehend *ease of execution* and *ease of circumstance*. Ease of execution is what our smartphones make possible every day by letting us see who's at the door with our smart doorbell, or by letting us order dinner from DoorDash in thirty seconds flat. It's technology as a utility to save time, money, or inconvenience. That's fine.

Ease of circumstance, however, is illusory. No smartphone can help us navigate a fight with our significant other, a child being bullied at school, a dying parent, fear over the outcome of an election or the changing climate, the anxiety of a medical diagnosis, or the stress of losing a job. Those are life circumstances in which reality is nonnegotiable and unimpressed by the power of even the niftiest app. They are times that require us to engage fully with others and with our own impressions and emotions, and technology is robbing us of those instincts.

Unintentionally, we are confusing execution and circumstance—applying the "there's got to be an app to fix this" sense to the real-world situations that can only be addressed with humanity, vulnerability, commitment, engagement, and attention—and that sometimes simply can't be solved. After all, that's what we are accustomed to. Because smart technology has made us so powerful, we are developing an unconscious sense that we are entitled to have things work out, to have even the most fraught crisis resolve with the tap of an app. When that doesn't happen—no app will ease a teenager's schoolyard shame over his shabby clothes or keep a grandparent with stage four cancer alive—we react with horror, even betrayal. We disengage. We close up shop. We quit. We Swipe.

We've come to feel, with unintended arrogance, that we're entitled to the Downhill portion of the Hamster Wheel, that thanks to smartphones and the cloud and Amazon Prime, life should be a series of easy ascents and great meals. We're forgetting the lesson that the beauty of being human often lies in the striving, in the dirt, in getting back up after a punch to the gut and continuing to fight until we win—bloody, but victorious. That makes Swiping inevitable. When even minor troubles or moments of friction are *in themselves* failures, what's the point of continuing with the marathon training or the great novel?

Distraction and Motivation—a Solution

There are no easy responses to this condition. The most reliable is the simplest but also the most difficult: cultivate hyperawareness of the difference between execution and circumstance, and to refuse the temptation to believe ourselves to be invulnerable because of the power that technology grants us. But achieving that level of metacognition and self-awareness is challenging.

The more realistic way to escape the perilous mindset created by technology's reality overlay might be to slay the twin demons of distraction and lack of motivation. In conducting online surveys for this book, the two most common reasons people cited for not finishing what they started were:

1. Life had too many distractions.
2. They didn't have the right motivation to sustain effort.

Sound familiar? In our modern lives, our near-addictive use of smartphones and similar tools renders it easier than ever to get lost in distraction. As for motivation, we lose it when the virtual wins that occur in the digital world—getting "likes," getting subscribers, landing a high score in an online game, scoring a great deal at an online retailer—overshadow the more difficult, more meaningful victories in the analog world, from sticking to a workout plan for two weeks to landing that coveted new job (or finding joy in our current workplace). To loosen the grip of technology on your self-efficacy and invite more beneficial uncertainty and surprise into your life, demote your smartphone. Make technology your second option for engaging with the world, not your first.

If distraction is an issue, engage with people and situations without technology as a crutch or advance scouting tool. You might be amazed at what this does to develop a connection—the "C" in MAGIC—to your environment or those around you. The most meaningful moments of our lives are neither safe nor comfortable. It's time we started relegating our smartphones and other tech back to the status they deserve: wonderful, nearly magical tools, but nothing more. They're not life.

CHAPTER 7

The Psychology of the Swipe

> The mind operates two parallel systems to navigate the world: System One, which is automatic and reflexive, requiring little or no conscious thought; and System Two, which requires attention, energy, choice, and analysis. System One leads us to Swipe in a reflexive effort to dodge discomfort.

Picture a pair of eyeglasses. As expressed in the saying "seeing the world through rose-colored glasses," these lenses color our worldview. One lens is continually etched by our life experiences. Those experiences might be positive—the birth of a child, landing that big job, enjoyable moments with family, acing an exam, finishing a 5K—or negative—serious health challenges, losing that perfect job, world crisis, personal betrayal, financial ruin.

These events could be exhilarating—that first jump from an airplane, a stellar score on the LSAT, your daughter's first soccer goal—but engraved on the same lens are also the tedious, mind-numbing activities that can leave you banging your head against the wall—a boring lecture, your coworker's incessant diatribe on why you should follow an underwater garlic colonic regimen, cleaning your apartment after your dog has shredded *another* roll of toilet paper in protest of you having the nerve to go to the gym, etc.

Then there's the other lens. It's tinted with your beliefs, desires, inspirations, and dreams. This lens is a representation of what you hold most precious. Inscribed into this lens may be your thoughts on family, beliefs on equal treatment for all, political orientation, a belief or disbelief in God, the worth and importance you place on an education, or even which college basketball team has your undying loyalty. This lens contains our values—from the Latin *valere*, meaning "to be of worth"—that which we consider to be most important or of greatest worth.

Each of these lenses—our experience lens and our values lens—colors how we see the world and, consequently, how we are likely to act. Our life experiences shape who we are and what we value. Similarly, our values affect how the events of our lives play out. You could even say that sitting through your neighbors' kid's last school performance of *The Scarlet Pimpernel* becomes a part of who you are and the way you see the world—though, hopefully, not a big part.

While most, if not all, of us would gladly grab a soft cloth and wipe away some of what coats these lenses, they are a part of who you are—a critical piece of what makes you, *you*. As we stated earlier, when we Swipe, as with Adam Sandler's reckless use of his magic remote control in *Click*, the Swipe *becomes* the experience.

When we Swipe often, instead of reflecting our experiences and values, those lenses become obscured by the effects of our Swipes. As Sandler's character learns too late in life, by disengaging from the uncomfortable parts of life, he has robbed himself and those around him of some of those very experiences, lessons, and emotions that he values most.

Country singer-songwriter Garth Brooks conveys this sentiment beautifully through the lyrics of "The Dance":

Yes, my life is better left to chance;
I could have missed the pain, but I'd have had to miss the dance.

Often life is more about the journey—the dance—than the destination. There is a good deal of evidence suggesting that we find happiness in our journey on days when we experience positive emotions—the high that comes from positive outcomes. That makes intuitive sense; we tend to be happy when good things happen. In a classic psychological study titled "Some Key Differences Between a Happy Life and Meaningful Life," however, social psychologist Roy Baumeister and colleagues found that while satisfying one's own immediate needs and wants resulted in temporary happiness, it had little relationship to a long-term, meaningful life.

Happiness, they found, was present-oriented, while *meaningfulness* involved integrating past, present, and future. Happiness was positively correlated to the frequency of positive experiences, while negatively correlated to the frequency of negative experiences.

That makes sense—the more positive experiences we have, the happier we tend to be. But interestingly, finding greater long-term meaning was related to a higher frequency of positive experiences *and* negative experiences.[1]

Wait a minute. We are happy when we have positive experiences, but a meaningful life comes through both positive *and* negative experiences? Well, yes.

Part of this also depends on the intensity of those life experiences. Let's go back to what we discussed in chapter 3 about intensity. Researchers Sean Murphy and Brock Bastian report in the *Journal of Positive Psychology* that the experiences we find most worthy of incorporating into our life story—the story of what makes us who we are—are often those that are most intense, not necessarily the experiences that give us the most pleasure.[2]

Pioneering psychologist Abraham Maslow was fascinated by this concept, and by what he referred to as "peak experiences."[3] He described these as "rare, exciting, oceanic, deeply moving, exhilarating, elevating experiences that generated an advanced form of perceiving reality, and are even mystic and magical in their effects." Maslow often pointed out how overcoming intense challenges and setbacks can be a key trigger for a peak experience.[4]

While Swiping past unpleasant experiences might provide us with temporary "happiness" by allowing us to dodge discomfort and our fear of failure, meaning in life comes from both positive and negative events. In particular, "peak experiences," whether positive or negative, create long-term meaningfulness. That's why, when you hear someone give a TED talk or see an Olympian profiled on television, the pivotal moments in their stories are often about overcoming hardships or setbacks. Such negative episodes become our peak experiences as we surmount obstacles, shaping our character and revealing both who we are and who we can become. As Sandler's character realized, Swiping robs us of the very experiences that make our lives meaningful. Every step in the dance matters, from the joyful parts to the painful stumbles.

The University Swipe

Over the past decade, we've instructed thousands of students in university settings. A favorite assignment is to have these bright young people create an "individual change project" in which they spend the four-month semester pursuing a form of personal change of their choosing. These changes are not to be a simple to-do list of goals. While "I want to lose fifteen pounds over five months" is a worthy goal, it is not a personal change for purposes of this assignment.

This is more what we have in mind: "My health is important to me. I am a person who prioritizes his health. A healthier lifestyle will allow me to do better in school, focus, feel more confident about myself, and live longer. I will become a healthy individual." While the goal is what the student wants to do, the change is who the student wants to become. Pretty cool, right?

You might expect a large percentage of students to choose projects related to health. After all, most of us have things like "lose weight" or "exercise more" on our perpetual to-do list, and with the pressures of school and social life, health often takes a back seat, even among the younger generation. But more than 65 percent of projects selected involve some variation of "I will be more focused and engaged so that I can accomplish what I *really* want to do." Some students want to focus on schoolwork. For others, this is about paying attention to family, friendships, or dating relationships. But what's most intriguing is not what the students hope to achieve with this kind of project but the reason they're frustrated with their level of focus and personal development in the first place:

They are constantly distracted, largely by technology.

Recently, while teaching in Europe, we become keenly aware of this when one intelligent, levelheaded grad student proposed her project. She began her presentation by asking her classmates, "If you had sixty-eight extra days in your year, what would you do with them?" The question generated some amusing responses and some sensible ones, and then the student revealed why she'd chosen that topic. "That's how much time I spend on social media each year," she said. "Sixty-eight days. I'd like to get those two months back." We may have been the only ones shocked by that observation, because the other students immediately nodded their heads as if to say, "I feel you, girl."

The next presenter had been using an iPhone app to track her mobile phone usage over the previous two weeks—no, the irony isn't lost on us. Her average personal cell phone use, excluding school and work, came to just under five hours per day. She hoped to reduce that to two. Again, no major reaction from her peers. They got it. They did the same thing.

These were international graduate students. Many would consider these individuals, most of whom spoke three or more languages fluently, to be some of the brightest young people on the planet. Yet that day was filled with expressions of guilt, shame, and even self-disgust as one by one they stood at the front of the classroom to hang their heads and confess they were unable to accomplish what they had hoped to in their busy lives because of distractions. Universally, social media was the chief villain.

We could launch into a self-righteous attack on evil technology and its enablement of the Swipe, and even point to social media as the leading cause,[5] but we beat that horse pretty thoroughly in chapter 6, so we'll refrain. Instead, let's focus on the curious revelations those students had. First, they saw that distractions were causing them to waste time and preventing them from engaging in what was "of greatest worth" to them, that which led to meaning and purpose. Second, they perceived what distractions were doing to their feelings of self-worth, sense of accomplishment, and basic mental well-being. Third, they weren't making progress toward what they held to be truly worthwhile. Growth and impact were hindered. Finally, in discussing the reasons for choosing to pick up their cell phones instead of doing something they knew would create greater meaning in the long run, each described this action in terms of some motive force beyond their control, pulling them away from achieving what mattered most. Most of these budding scholars first lamented the wasted time and then quickly turned to the fact that each believed they were missing out on key experiences.

We live in a world of constant distraction. In their work, Harvard psychologists Matthew Killingsworth and Daniel Gilbert found that nearly half of our waking hours are spent thinking about something other than other than what we are doing. This constant mind-wandering is making us unhappy. They write, "A human mind is a wandering mind, and a wandering mind is an unhappy mind. The ability to think about what is not happening is a cognitive achievement that comes at an emotional cost."

The two researchers developed an iPhone app that contacted 2,250 individuals at random intervals throughout their day to ask how happy they were, what they were doing at the time, and what they were thinking about—the current activity or something else. They found that 46.9 percent of the time the study subjects were thinking about something other than the activity in which they were immediately engaged.

"Mind-wandering is an excellent predictor of people's happiness," they wrote. "In fact, how often our minds leave the present and where they tend to go is a better predictor of our happiness than the activities in which we are engaged."[6]

Can't Make Up My Mind(s)

As noted *Grit* author Angela Duckworth writes, "Some would argue that human attention, not money, is the most valuable commodity there is. It's the ultimate scarce resource."[7] With this precious resource often squandered in cyberspace, why is it we are so inclined to Swipe to an activity or preoccupation other than what is currently in front of us?

The answer may be more complicated than simply having the willpower to concentrate on getting things done. Turning to the field of cognitive psychology may show us, at least, how we got here. Psychologist, economist, and 2002 Nobel laureate Daniel Kahneman gives us some brilliant insight into this reaction through what he refers to as "Two Minds."[8] An example:

Looking at a picture of a young, dark-haired woman, note her angry expression. You sense that this anger will cause her to say something unkind, likely in a loud voice. The thought about what she would do next came automatically to your mind. You don't know anything about her personality, other than what you see in front of you. Yet the picture prompted you to anticipate future events—she was angry; therefore she was about to say something unkind. You did not have think about what she would do. It came effortlessly and unintentionally to your mind.

Now consider the following mathematical problem posed by Kahneman: 17 x 24. You knew immediately that the solution involved multiplication—you did not have to think about it. You probably knew you could solve it with a paper and pencil or with a calculator. You also likely recognized that both 12,609 and 123 were not plausible responses, but that the answer likely fit somewhere between those two numbers. At this point, you can make a conscious choice whether to complete the problem or not to bother with it. If you decided to solve the problem, it took time and effort to do so.

In confronting the multiplication task, you accessed the portion of your memory that detailed the steps of solving a multiplication problem. The process required mental work—deliberate, slow, intentional, and ordered effort. If you chose to compute the product, the computation not only involved your mind but your body as well. Your body tensed, your blood pressure rose, your heart rate increased, and your pupils dilated. When you found the solution (408), your physical state returned to normal.

What is the difference between these two thought processes? In the first example of the angry woman, we used what Kahneman refers to as "System One thinking." System One ("thinking fast") operates with little or no conscious effort. System Two ("thinking slow") enabled you to process the math problem. System Two allocates attention and cognitive resources to mental activities that demand them, such as mathematical problems or other problems that require choice, attention, and focused concentration.

System One thinking is generally involuntary. If we were to say, "Two plus two equals . . ." you would respond, "Four," without thinking about it. The response didn't require complex thinking. In fact, it was most likely a part of your everyday language. But have you ever heard someone toss off, "You know, seventeen times twenty-four equals four hundred eight," when hanging out with a group of friends? Unlikely. Solving the second problem is not reflexive; it involves voluntary attention and thought.

Systems One and Two reflect the path from conscious to unconscious competence. When we first learn something, even "$2 + 2 = 4$" in kindergarten, it demands conscious effort. But after a period of time, and through learning and achieving mastery, what was once voluntary becomes involuntary, requiring limited thought. It is now reflexive, automatic. You can probably drive from your home to your place of work—and back—without thinking about it because you've done it so many times. System One handles that task. This is why when we drive routes over and over again we often can't remember exiting, stopping at three traffic lights, or turning off the engine. That's also why, after a route becomes familiar, we can engage in important phone conversations—hands-free, please—while safely reaching our destination. System One is in control of the vehicle, so System Two is free to carry on a complex, nuanced conversation.

When we master a complex task, it ceases to be complex. We are on autopilot. Moving from playing a basic C major scale on the piano to mastering Chopin concerti becomes reflexive with sustained practice. That's virtuosity. What once required attention and labored System Two calculations has become a series of System One events that we do without thinking. But complexity is relative. Above we should have said that when we master a complex task it ceases to be complex—for us. For someone just learning to drive or learning the piano, the most basic tasks can be extremely challenging, requiring considerable cognitive resources.

Most of us would like to believe we are System Two driven. We tell ourselves that we dedicate thought and effort to considering what is before us, analyzing the data and making deliberate choices with the information we have. We think of ourselves as reasonable, logical individuals whose choices are based on the values and beliefs on those eyeglass lenses. To be fair, this is partially true. Both systems are always active and available whenever we are awake. In this area, however, we are also somewhat self-deluded.

System One runs automatically. System Two is also running all the time, but it remains in low-energy mode until summoned. System One is the first line of defense, generating suggestions, impressions, and ideas for System Two. System Two makes choices as needed. Most of the time, however, System Two adopts the suggestions that System One makes, with few modifications. These suggestions turn into beliefs and actions.

When System One cannot solve the problem or provide an answer, it hollers for System Two to help out and supply processing horsepower. System Two also kicks in when something happens that violates the way System One views the world, such as seeing someone or something out of its normal or expected context, or upon receiving surprising information that requires deeper processing. Suppose you've driven to work via the same route for eight years and can navigate on autopilot. But one day a major construction project closes your usual route, and you're forced to detour into neighborhoods and use roads you know nothing about. System One can't help you. You need to draw on your knowledge of your area, street layout, and traffic patterns. This is a job for System Two!

Bottom line, while System Two monitors our deeper behavior, most of what we see and do originates with System One because that system draws on fewer processing resources. It's our brain conserving energy. System Two has the final say when things become complex or difficult.

Most of the time, the relationship between these complimentary systems hums along nicely. System One is highly efficient. Most of its predictions are accurate. It has excellent recall of past events, experiences, outcomes, and situations. Its responses are quick; however, this pairing isn't a perfect solution. System One sometimes answers questions it shouldn't—questions that are better suited to the complex analytical power of System Two. System One is also a creature of habit; it operates on biases. And that, young Jedi, is where the Swipe comes in.

Two Systems and a Swipe

System One is territorial. If it can keep System Two out of the loop, it will. Meanwhile, System Two, while a workhorse, is lazy. If System One can handle the situation, System Two is content to kick back, put its feet up, grab the TV remote, and stay out of the way. Much of the time, System One makes short work of complex challenges by relying on the brain's archives of habit and patterned response. We encounter a situation, and System One queries, "What worked the last time we ran into this?" Synapses fire, and in a microsecond the archives deliver the answer. System One says, "Cool. Let's do that again." Most of the time, this resolves the situation with the least difficulty and in the least time.

If relying on habits, patterns, and biases doesn't get the job done, System One either moves away from the situation or throws it over the wall to System Two. But System One knows that if it has to call on System Two there will be an energy cost—it takes some work to solve the 17 x 24 problem. The more challenging the problem, the more energy needed.

As mentioned in chapter 1, in Sigmund Freud's psychoanalytic theory of personality, also known as the pleasure-pain principle, the pleasure principle—Freud refers to this as the id—strives to fulfill our most basic urges: hunger, thirst, comfort, emotion, and sex. Freud believed that during our earliest years the id controls our behavior. Children react not based out of logic but out of impulse, as any parent of a four-year-old—or most teens, for that matter—could tell you. No problem, when we're kids. A quick reprimand, and we're back on our merry, oblivious way.

But that doesn't work when we grow into adults. As we become more emotionally and physically developed, our ability to control these impulses steps in—Freud calls this character the ego. It doesn't mean those childish impulses are not present; they are always with us. Most of us have simply learned to control them and put them into context. Doing so is the price of admission to civilized society—that is, until we *don't* control them.

System One is the system of the id. It operates out of impulse and quick reaction. It is involuntary—we're not making conscious choices. Instead, System One compels actions based on past events: *hot stove = burned finger = remove hand now!* Because of this hold-over from our early lives, we're always seeking to remove sensory displeasure and mental discomfort from our lives—not consciously but reactively and sometimes illogically.

NERD ALERT!

Stanford psychologist Albert Bandura developed the theory of self-efficacy.[9] Self-efficacy is an individual's belief in their ability to succeed in a particular situation. It is an individual's belief in that they can accomplish what they intend to accomplish. Bandura posited that individuals confronting their fears of failure—Bandura focused much of his work on phobias—would have a higher degree of self-efficacy the next time these fears were manifest. To test his theory, Bandura assembled participants, all afraid of snakes, into two groups. One group would interact directly with their phobia (snakes), while the other group would merely observe others' interactions with snakes. The results showed that those who interacted directly with the snakes showed a higher degree of self-efficacy, as well as a lesser degree of avoidance the next time they encountered snakes than did the group who merely observed.[10]

Out of the Comfort Zone

Mental discomfort can take many forms, as we have already discussed. It can manifest as emotional or even physical pain—stomach cramps due to anxiety, for example. It might be the result of current stress or of *anticipatory* stress, the discomfort that comes from what *might* happen. It may be the result of a perceived loss of control, or a perceived lack of knowledge or training in something you're being asked to do. It may be the outcome of facing two or more conflicting goals. In today's action-packed, instant-gratification world, boredom could even be considered discomfort. The causes and types of discomfort are nearly endless.

The cure-all for these many forms of discomfort is the Swipe, an involuntary, thoughtless action that allows us to escape or disengage from the source of our discomfort. Incidentally, the mechanism that compels us to make a mad dash away from what's stressing us out applies whether or not we're trying to finish something arduous; it's universal. It's a System One action, with no choice or decision involved. We're psychologically and physiologically primed to retreat from discomfort as expeditiously as possible when it arises, so we do.

If I can disengage from a situation I find unpleasant, emotionally negative, physically or mentally taxing, anxiety ridden, or just plain boring, I can get immediate relief from these negative feelings—and perhaps even replace them with a temporary positive feeling—by Swiping. Without thought of consequences, System One defaults to the easiest, most pleasurable outcome.

As we've also mentioned, there are some positive psychological reasons for the Swipe. A Swipe may temporarily remove us from a stressful situation. As the world presents us with so many decisions, a Swipe means we don't have to burden ourselves, for the moment, with making those stressful decisions, where System Two would have to expend energy. But this mechanism is more complex than simply saying, "I quit," or exchanging temporary discomfort for momentary pleasure, and it's not really very effective at achieving the results we desire.

Formerly known in psychology terms as *avoidance*, the tendency to flee from the "real world," or what is in front of us, is known in psychologyspeak as *escapism*. Rather than helping to relieve high-stress situations, escapism has been found to increase symptoms of psychological disorder, such as depression.[11]

Do you Swipe on things you find pleasant or easy? No. This reinforces an important point. In Swiping, we don't always switch our attention to something that has no value. In other words, Swiping doesn't always mean we're wasting time. As you sit down to write that first novel for the sixth time, perhaps you remember that you need to get the mail. And feed the dog. And check the expiration date on your dairy products. And whatever else. Those may not be bad activities, and really not wasted time. But engaging in them is also not allowing you to accomplish what you intended to accomplish. And there goes your progress and the impact you might have had on what was more important to you.

Because of this, our *intention* often defines whether or not an action is a Swipe. Are you getting up to grab the mail because you genuinely need to see if you've received your past-due vehicle registration? That's not a Swipe. But if you're getting up because doing so breaks your engagement in a task that's provoking discomfort in you, despite the fact that you deeply want to complete it, you are Swiping. It's a fine line. We love to feel a sense of accomplishment. Because we *can* often be successful in the pursuits we Swipe to, we feel better about ourselves, having at least accomplished *something*.

At times, when we know a bar will be hard for us to clear, System One will substitute a lesser, often more temporary objective—clear my desk and reorganize my desk supplies—for the harder task— finish writing chapter 6. This Swipe allows us to feel a sense of immediate accomplishment and completion, but it does nothing to help us achieve that more difficult task that might bring us a peak experience.

Here we see that there is often a conflict between what is on our values lens and what we act upon. This is known as the *value-action gap*, or *intention-action gap*, and it occurs when one's values, attitudes, or intentions don't match their actions.

HOW NOT TO SWIPE

When we Swipe, we reflexively pivot away from an activity because of psychological or emotional distress, taking up a distraction that relieves that distress. But what if one way to short-circuit the Swipe was to take the reflex out of the picture—to make dropping the activity intentional and temporary? Picture a busy chef. In an hour, she might dash from her cooktop, where she's poaching scallops, to the oven, where a dessert tart is baking, to the soup station to check on the temperature of a bisque, to conferring with the head waiter, and then back to the scallops, multiple times. Despite her divided attention, each dish winds up cooked to perfection. She's choosing to step away from one activity to engage in another, and then circling back to reengage. We call this the "Swipe-switch." Instead of an either-or proposition—work on a desired goal that provokes discomfort or relieve the discomfort with a handful of trivial distractions—the Swipe-switch blends the two intentionally. How to do it:

1. Set yourself up to work on a desirable but difficult goal, such as writing or exercising. A chef would refer to this action by the term *mise en place*, a French culinary phrase meaning to "put in place" or "to gather." Prior to cooking, the chef will prepare and organize the equipment and ingredients he or she will use. This term has also spilled into psychology, referring to preparing for thought or action beforehand.[12]

2. Choose three to four secondary activities that are easier but also reasonably productive: sweeping the

floor, paying bills, finishing the next chapter in the book you're reading, etc.

3. Set a time limit for how long you will work on your big goal—say, thirty minutes—and start. Set an alarm on your phone to keep yourself honest.

4. When you reach that time limit, set your big project aside, no matter where you are. Even if things are going well, even if you're in flow, stop.

5. Switch to one of your more trivial tasks for fifteen minutes.

6. Go back to your big task. Repeat.

The Swipe-switch changes the game by using conscious choice to make System One less important. Rather than disengaging from your desirable goal reactively because you're uncomfortable, you're doing so predictably and intentionally. You have control. Then, by engaging in less demanding tasks, you allow your discomfort to dissipate before reengaging.

Mind the Gap

Swiping means we don't make a decision. We don't choose. System One has already reacted for us. No decision. No discomfort. No emotion. No stress. For now. Until System Two is left with the fallout, that is.

Back to our university students. Most were clearly aware that their lack of focus was a result of the Swipe. System One had kicked in and made their decisions for them, without them thinking about why they were acting or the consequences of that action; however, while their initial Swipe of picking up their phones was intentional, the outcome was not.

Each Swipe was intended only as a short-term escape, not a five-hour venture. Initially, most of the students hopped on the internet for one or more of the following reasons—or so they told themselves:

- A quick check-in with friends.
- They wanted to blow off some steam before diving into their assigned papers.
- They hoped to relax a bit before tackling the mountain of tasks ahead of them.
- It was a habit—get home, check the phone, use the bathroom, get in bed, check the phone, wake up, check the phone, repeat.

For the most part, they hadn't intended to Swipe. It was a reflex either based on habit or on temporary avoidance. System One stepped in and drove their actions based on impulse and reaction. Unfortunately, that "quick check-in" frequently ended up lasting much longer than they intended, sometimes until the early morning hours, and often without the students realizing what had occurred. Before they knew it, "just one TikTok view" and "just one Instagram post" had consumed an entire evening—and then, eventually, sixty-eight days out of the year. The value-action gap between what they *intended* to accomplish and what they *did* accomplish was huge. Cue the guilt, shame, and regret over things left undone.

This phenomenon, which we call *attention asymmetry*—a seemingly small shift in attention leads to outsized consequences—highlights the dangers of Swiping. While the Swipe may be the product of a momentary impulse without intention, the fallout of that impulse can become a long-term trip down a distraction rabbit hole that derails us from the important things we need to do—in this case, the vital university studies and research that these students needed to complete their advanced degrees.

Based in part on these effects, many so-called experts claim that excessive screen time results in impaired mental health, particularly for teens and millennials. This may be true; however, the issue is not always social media, according to psychologists. In fact, an eight-year Brigham Young University study of teens showed that an increase in the amount of time spent on social networking sites did not increase the levels of depression or anxiety.[13] So why did these university students feel they were so negatively affected by spending hours on their smartphones? Perhaps the answer can be summarized in one student's statement:

> Spending 40 percent of my waking hours diving into social media means that's time I'm not doing what is most important to me, what I value most in my life. I'm a social person. Wouldn't it make more sense to spend time connecting with my family and friends face-to-face and in real time versus "communicating" with them through low-quality photos or videos, memes, and short texts? I also don't ever finish what I wanted to do. Or, when I do, it is through a lot of last-minute stress because I've put it off. I end up feeling bad about myself, comparing myself to others, not getting done what I wanted to do, and losing focus when I'm in class because I'm too tired, or I'm constantly thinking about checking my phone. At the end of the day, I haven't gotten anything out of class, and I'm disengaged in school. It may feel good to pick up my phone now, but I always end up feeling bad about myself.

In other words, Swiping. Another student, a lively young lady, described the problem this way:

> The smartphone is a great invention. It offers many possibilities that make life easier. But my smartphone has a very negative impact on me. I actually get cramps in my hand and forearm. My eyes are always dry and red from staring at my screen. I lose a lot of time scrolling through apps. I could finish things much faster and have way more time for other activities. I have a guilty conscience, full of regret, because I wasted so much time on my mobile phone. Knowing that once again I have chosen the path of least resistance by being on social media instead of getting things done on my to-do list leaves me feeling uncomfortable. I lose valuable sleep time. It is a brain drain. I see this spilling into other areas of my life now.

Ouch.

These students are correct. Researchers have clearly shown that the mere presence of a smartphone might reduce cognitive capacity, even when we are able to avoid checking our devices.[14] Perhaps more important, however, was the fact that being on their phones caused them to not accomplish what they intended to accomplish. This, in turn, left them feeling less confident and more guilt ridden. Ultimately, they Swiped from temporary discomfort to long-term dissatisfaction and reduced self-confidence. The tasks they needed to check off the list didn't go away; they were merely postponed. They still had to be done. But now there was a painful valley between the initial Swipe and the final accomplishment of the tasks, a chasm filled with wasted time, neglected relationships, negative self-talk, and regret. You can see how this might have affected their "MAGIC."

To make matters worse, the effects of attention asymmetry spill over to other areas of life. A study of 774 college students examined student use of technology such as social media, texting, emailing, search engines, and instant messaging. The study assessed not only performance in the classroom but outside the classroom as well. Results showed that the students who were commonly involved in these technology-focused activities while in the classroom ended up with significantly lower grade point averages than their peers. No big *aha* moment there.

Quite surprising, however, was the finding that students involved in technology multitasking in the classroom also tended to engage more frequently in high-risk behaviors outside the classroom, including increased drinking, smoking, marijuana use, and illegal drug use. They were also more likely to engage in binge drinking, drink and drive, ride in a car driven by others who had been drinking, get into fights, and have multiple sex partners over the previous thirty days.[15] In other words, reckless pleasure-seeking behavior. So, in addition to a graveyard of failed attempts and partially completed projects, other areas of their lives were also affected negatively.

The Power of Regret

In his 2022 book, *The Power of Regret*, Daniel Pink details the result of his study, the "American Regret Project." Pink's team asked 4,489 people to respond to the question: "How often do you look back on your life and wish you had done things differently?" Only 1 percent of respondents said they never engaged in such behavior. About 17 percent indicated that they did so rarely, with 43 percent doing so frequently. Overall, 82 percent of respondents said that looking back with regret was at least occasionally part of their lives, making Americans more likely to experience some form of regret than to floss.[16]

Pink also cites research spanning the past forty years. Social scientist Susan Shimanoff conducted studies on conversations with both undergraduates and married couples. Shimanoff's team analyzed these everyday conversations, transcribed them, and reviewed the transcripts for themes. She then compiled a list of both positive and negative emotions frequently mentioned throughout the conversations. The most common negative emotion was regret, which was also the second most common emotion overall, second only to love.[17]

When we Swipe, we are often left with remorse, disappointment, and regret. Regret is real and can have long-term effects on well-being.[18] Often regret doesn't pass quickly; it can last days, months, or a lifetime. Dealing with regret is even more difficult because of the other negative emotions connected to it: guilt, sorrow, and helplessness. Not only can regret affect our emotional health but it can have tremendous impact on our physical well-being as well.[19]

According to J. Kim Penberthy, professor of psychiatry and neurobehavioral sciences at UVA Health in Charlottesville, Virginia, there are two ways to experience regret: the *action* path and the *inaction* path. We can regret the things we did, or we can regret the things we did not do. Action-related regrets often cause individuals to learn from their mistakes and move on. Regret related to inaction—those things we did not do or opportunities we have lost—is more likely to lead to depression or anxiety. It is a sense of "stuckness," as Penberthy calls it, a "feeling of longing over not knowing what could have been."[20]

In the case of these students, and most of us, System One makes a rapid-fire evaluation of what is in front of us. Without a conscious thought on our part, System One puts an action plan in place, with no consideration of long-term effects. Similar to the *hot stove = burned finger = move hand* neuromotor response, we don't involve the parts of the brain required to make more complex decisions. Rather than invoking System Two in a decision about "What do I need to do to get this thesis completed by the deadline?" System One has already made that decision for us out of habit. In picking up the cell phone, "just to check on my email," we deny System Two the chance to plan a strategy to reach that long-term goal. Enter regret.

You might not be a student. But it's likely there are many instances in your life in which System One has made the decision to Swipe for you, without you even being aware: working out, dealing with coworkers or subordinates, facing complex work projects, having difficult conversations with your spouse or children, and so on. Because of the Swipe, System Two remains oblivious to the task before you.

The result: You take a detour and fail to accomplish what you had intended to accomplish. Each of the five elements of MAGIC suffers, and you disengage even further. As illustrated by the Hamster Wheel, this is cyclical; we repeat the behavior. The beliefs, values, and dreams on your "lens" don't get translated into action and experiences, because you don't get to the place where you can make that choice. Distraction robs you of the pleasures of accomplishment that come through perseverance, determination, hard work, and learning.

We'll talk more about distractions and the brain in the next chapter. Focus up.

CHAPTER 8

The Swipe and the Brain

Distraction is not some benign force, an annoying fly buzzing around our consciousness. It's a threat to our ability to focus our attention, and thus to bring our intellect and talents to bear in getting the things we want most.

It sounds like an intro to a bad joke: "A German, a Finn, and an American walk onto a basketball court . . ." With just half a second remaining in the game, and the NBA's Washington Wizards leading the Chicago Bulls by a narrow 98–96 margin, an inbound pass from seven-foot Bulls forward Lauri Markkanen to shooting guard Zach LaVine resulted in a tangle of arms under the net and a foul charged to Wizards small forward Isaac Bonga, drawing a piercing whistle. The violation sends LaVine to the free-throw line.

Calling a questionable play like this is a serious matter for rookie NBA referee Jenna Schroeder. "All the pressure in the world I felt like was on me," Schroder told MLive reporter Lauren Williams.

"And I'm just a rookie trying not to screw up, and that's when I'm like, 'OK, I'm in the NBA.'"[1]

Schroeder also grabbed the attention of NBA fans as they noted her impressive speed in a viral *SportsCenter* tweet of a Lakers-Grizzlies matchup, where she outran several of the athletes on the court.[2] But perhaps even more impressive is the fact that Schroeder is the sixth-ever woman chosen to referee in the male-only NBA. But let's turn away from Schroeder's gender and toward the marvel that is her brain—all our brains, really.

Mind and Body

Like her fellow athletes on the court, Schroeder's body reacts quickly to the physical demands of the game. Cardiorespiratory systems increase activity; digestive systems slow down. Blood pressure increases as heart rates increase. Adrenaline levels rise as adenosine triphosphate (ATP) creates energy from food through conversion to adenosine diphosphate (ADP), stimulating the heart to beat faster.

The diaphragm increases oxygen flow by up to fifteen times. The burning of glycogen and oxygen increases body temperature, and two million sweat glands produce as much as 1.4 liters of sweat per hour as the body works to cool itself. Capillaries open, increasing blood flow to the brain by up to twenty times.

As a power forward decides whether to drive to the baseline or pull up and shoot, a complex web of connections through his brain make quick decisions involving rapid coordination between the premotor cortex and the prefrontal cortex. With neural signals traveling through the brain at an impressive 268 miles per hour,[3] the athlete must make his decision to change direction within 100 milliseconds if this change of mind is to succeed in altering his physical actions.

Neuroscientists at Johns Hopkins University found that if that decision takes more than two hundred milliseconds the original decision will have already been put in motion—the signal to move the foot and handle the basketball will already be traveling to the muscles.[4] If the player makes the split-second decision to pull up and shoot, rather than drive to the hoop as he had originally intended, he cannot stop his action if that decision is made even just a few milliseconds too late.

The human brain—all fourteen hundred grams (about three pounds) of it—contains between eighty-six billion[5] and one hundred billion neurons.[6] That's comparable to the number of stars in the Milky Way. Each neuron in our brain performs computations at an incredibly rapid pace, clocked in milliseconds—thousandths of a second.

Our brain's integration of lightning-fast processing and immense storage is staggering. We identify and sort through what seems an impossible mountain of complex stimuli in fractions of a second. Over the course of a lifetime, our brain stores fifty thousand times more information than is housed in the Library of Congress.[7] If each neuron had only the ability to store, say, one memory—we really don't know how to calculate the size of a memory—that would amount to just a few gigabytes of storage space—less than the iPod you had back in 2010. Each neuron forms connections to other neurons, resulting in over one hundred trillion neural connections,[8] giving your brain's memory capacity something closer to around 2.5 petabytes of data. By comparison, the average 4K movie is about 100GB. One petabyte of storage could hold eleven thousand 4K movies; it would take more than 2.5 years of nonstop binge-watching to get through just one petabyte of movie data.[9] Small wonder that neuroscientists consider the human brain to be the most complex object in the universe.[10]

"Perhaps the most impressive feat of the human brain is its functional offspring the human mind," write neuroscientists Adam Gazzaley and Larry Rosen in their book, *The Distracted Mind: Ancient Brains in a High-Tech World*. The mind is "the essence of every emotion you feel, every thought you have, every sensation you experience, every decision you make, every move you take, every word you utter. In the truest sense, [the mind] is who you are."[11]

Fascinating. Yet somehow we still can't remember where we parked the car.

NERD ALERT!

You've heard this statistic: "We only use 10 percent of our brains." The idea is the subject of Hollywood tropes in movies like *Lucy* and *Limitless*. Really? Why aren't we doing more? Maybe the miscited belief that neurons make up about 10 percent of all cells in the brain might be one of the reasons for the notion that we use just 10 percent of our brain capacity.[12] Actually, we use 100 percent of our brain, or at least some of us do. Neurologists agree that the brain is always active, with millions of neurons rapidly firing away, even when we're sleeping.[13]

Do I Have Your Attention?

Back to the NBA and referee Jenna Schroeder. While we are willing to shell out fifty bucks for a nosebleed seat on the top row to watch some of the best athletes in the world duke it out on the court, the forgotten star of each game may be the referee—the one who's considered to do her best work when we don't even notice her on the floor. Consider this: In his best season of shooting, the great Michael Jordan sank 53.9 percent of his shots from the field. In comparison, an NBA ref averages around five hundred calls, or no-calls, in a single game, with an accuracy rate between 93 and 95 percent.[14]

What really makes this extraordinary is that everything around our referee vies for her attention. The movement of the ball. The lines on the court. The rim. Angry fans, angry players. The pain in her ankle. The two opponents under the basket, jostling for the inbound pass as the small forward topples over in an obvious flop to try and draw a charging foul. Not to mention the guy behind the backboard waving the foam worms, sitting next to his buddy who sneaked in the homemade vuvuzela.

Fifty percent of the referee's brain is dedicated to just one responsibility: visual perception. Her field of view is approximately 200 degrees, with the spot of best acuity directly in the center of her field of view. In that 2 percent of her 360-degree circle, she has twenty-twenty vision—and nowhere else.

To illustrate this point, professor of psychology and contemplative neuroscience Dr. Amishi P. Jha proposes a miniexperiment: Extend both arms fully in front of you, holding up both thumbs so that they touch side to side. The width of your two thumbnails together represents about two degrees, where your visual acuity is highest. Now move your thumbs apart. Clarity fades until your eyes dart back and forth between thumbnails in order to reposition one of the thumbs in that narrow 2 percent band.[15]

"Everything around us is competing for brain activity at all times," states Dr. Jha. "Attention biases brain activity. Whatever it is you pay attention to will have more neural activity associated with it.

Your attention, quite literally, alters the function of your brain at the cellular level."[16]

All this factors into that potentially game-changing call on the court. Here's the kicker—it's not just everything around the official on the hardwood that wants her attention; it's also what's *not* around her.

To illustrate, let's try a quick self-assessment. During the past five minutes, while you've been reading, has that miraculous mind of yours disengaged from this book? How about in the last two minutes? The last sixty seconds? Was there a moment when you tuned out and thought about work, where you're going for dinner, or where you left your car keys, before you shook yourself and resumed reading? Go on, answer honestly. We won't be offended.

Actually, we already know the answer. It's yes. Of course you did.

Our brains are extraordinarily vulnerable to momentary, involuntary deviations of attention—it's just how we're built. We're distracted up to 50 percent of the time—minds wandering, not fully present, disengaged, and mentally absent from what is in front of us. Numerous studies tell us that a wandering mind is a part of everyday life,[17, 18] even during the performance of experimental tasks designed to measure our ability to focus.[19] Across these studies, the rates of mind-wandering range from 30 to 50 percent of our waking hours. Some forms of this unfocused mental activity, such as daydreaming, are even beneficial.[20]

Now try to refocus. Close your eyes and take ten deep, even breaths. Focus *only* on your breathing—in, out, in, out. As soon as your focus strays away from your breathing, stop and open your eyes. The exercise should take less than a minute. Start . . . now.

Elevator music plays . . .

Not easy, is it? How many breaths did you manage before your hyperactive mind turned to something outside your breathing? Ten? Unless you're an experienced mindfulness meditator, not a chance. If you got two or three breaths in before your thoughts flipped to something else, you did very well.

What distracted you? Was it external—a car passing, the buzz of lights, someone talking, your uncomfortable chair? Or was it internal—thinking about not being distracted; remembering you have an appointment later today; thinking, *This is a pointless exercise. I have better things to do?* Most likely it was a combination of both kinds of distraction that pulled your focus elsewhere before you got deep into the exercise.

Jha and her colleagues conducted a lab study in which they tasked undergraduate students with sitting at computers, silently reading chapters from a psychology textbook. Students were encouraged to pay close attention, as they could receive course credit after they took a quiz. The text was presented one sentence at a time on the screen, and the students pressed the space bar to advance to the next sentence. Most of the text flowed naturally, except for an occasional out-of-context string, which occurred about 5 percent of the time. If students were paying attention, they would notice the displaced sentence and press the shift key instead of the space bar.

A quiz, course credit, pay attention, push some keys—simple task with a decent reward. Yet students missed the out-of-context sentences the majority of the time, and most failed to retain the material.

Jha's team, as well as others, have repeated this experiment—and variations of it—many times. Participants fail to recognize the sentences are meaningless about 30 percent of the time,[21] pressing the space bar rather than the tab key an average of seventeen times before they realize what they are reading makes no sense.[22]

We all struggle to maintain our attention, even when the consequences for losing focus could be disastrous. In April 2013, the US Air Force stripped seventeen officers based in Minot, North Dakota, of their ability to control and launch nuclear missiles after the group failed a test of its missile launch procedures.[23] Later that year, the Associated Press broke a story about air force officers napping while leaving open a blast door intended to prevent intruder access to an underground missile command post.[24] All of this came just five years after CNN reported that three crew members had been disciplined for falling asleep while in control of a classified electronic part containing launch codes for intercontinental nuclear missiles.[25]

Jha found similar dismal results in her student lab studies. There were zero circumstances under which participants maintained focus 100 percent of the time. They drifted, even when instructed, motivated, required, paid, or rewarded to focus. This isn't just students pushing keys while struggling to stay alert reading a psychology text, one sentence at a time. It's not just weary air force officers. Studies across multiple disciplines, backgrounds, job roles, and tasks report similar findings.[26] At some point in our day—at multiple points in our day, actually—we all disengage.

Our brains are mind-bogglingly susceptible to distraction. We disengage quickly. Even when we are physically present, we often are mentally absent. And when we disengage, we are more likely to remain disengaged, become discouraged, and Swipe.

The Distraction Plague

Written between 700 and 800 BC, the *Odyssey* tells Homer's tale of Trojan War hero Odysseus, also known as Ulysses. As Odysseus and his men sail home to the island of Ithaca, the goddess Circe warns his about the Sirens—beautiful enchantresses with an irresistible song who will distract him from his path as they pass by. As the account goes, a sailor caught up in the songs of the Sirens suffers death, their remains piled in great bone heaps at the Sirens' side.

Odysseus heeds Circe's warning, instructing his men to insert wax plugs into their ears as the ship nears the island of the Sirens, deafening them from the Sirens' song. Still, curiosity and ego lead Odysseus to ignore his own instructions, and he opts to listen to the Sirens' enchanting melodies. He orders his men to restrain him by binding him to the ship's mast so he cannot follow the song to his doom.

As the ship approaches the island, the song drives Odysseus mad with the desire to follow its call, and he orders his men to release him. But having received previous instruction to cover their ears and leave Odysseus bound, his men do not hear him and ignore his pleas. With their captain bound to the mast, the ship sails past the Sirens, whose song continues to deceive Odysseus with promises of knowledge, peace, and the secrets of the world. As the crew passes the island, their ears choked off to the Sirens' incantations, they realize that these mermaids of alleged beauty—half woman, half bird—are actually hideous, monstrous creatures with vicious, crooked claws, set only on the crew's destruction.

Homer's tale is a parable for the many alluring physical and mental distractions we face today, each promising us wisdom and the secrets of the world. But before we go further, let's define what we mean by *distraction*. It's easy to think of distraction as something momentary and benign, like the tone of a smartphone notification that pulls us away from something we're reading, or someone in the break room laughing loudly while we're trying to compose an email. And individually, most distractions are tiny, seconds-long interruptions of our attention. Cumulatively, however, they add up to an hours-long theft of the focus and motivation we require in order to achieve even small goals. At scale, distractions consume our time and mental energy with trifles and render us blind to the issues that we see as our highest priorities, such as family, social justice, personal growth, or our life's mission.

Distraction, in other words, is a big deal.

The trouble is, distraction is also a constant factor in modern life. Distractions impair our ability to focus on our goals, our relationships, our work, what and where we eat, and even our driving. In fact, the US National Highway Traffic Safety Administration reported that fatalities in distraction-affected crashes increased by 9.9 percent from 2018 to 2019, while speeding-related fatalities, alcohol-impaired-driving fatalities, and drowsy-driving deaths *decreased* during that same time by 1.1 percent, 5.3 percent, and 11.2 percent, respectively.[27]

The father of modern psychology, William James, described our minds as fleeting birds:

> Our mental life, like a bird's life, seems to be made of an alternation of flights and perchings. The rhythm of language expresses this, where every thought is expressed in a sentence, and every sentence closed by a period. The resting-places are usually occupied by sensorial imaginations of some sort, whose peculiarity is that they can be held before the mind for an indefinite time, and contemplated without changing; the places of flight

are filled with thoughts of relations, static or dynamic, that for the most part obtain between the matters contemplated in the periods of comparative rest.[28]

Look at the phrase "paying attention." Language has evolved to reflect the reality that in order accomplish anything we must "spend" our attention, expending mental energy to focus our minds on what we desire. Attention is currency. It's valuable. Why else would advertisers try to "capture" our attention? We "lend" our attention to others briefly because it has value, and because without it, nothing intentional can occur. Attention is the mental tool we use to impose our will upon the physical world.

In our magnificent brains, the attention system has developed to filter out the unnecessary distractions competing for focus. An important component of focus is the reticular activating system (RAS), a bundle of nerves in your brain stem. Among its other functions, including regulating the autonomic nervous system, the RAS, along with other parts of our brain, acts as a sort of information filter, determining which incoming information you perceive consciously and which data is sent to your unconscious mind, which has far greater processing capacity than the conscious mind, for storage and analysis.[29] One example of the RAS at work is the phenomenon known as the "new-car paradox," in which immediately after you buy a new car, as you drive around, you suddenly notice all the other people driving the same car you just purchased. Where were all those other Teslas before? They were always there, but your conscious mind didn't register their presence, because they weren't relevant to you. Now they are.

The RAS—and the other brain circuitry controlling attention— keeps our conscious mind from being overloaded, paralyzed, and unable to act. This system is constantly active, with everything around us competing for a sliver of our attention. Its filtering function is critical. As with our NBA referee, we cannot possibly process all the information bombarding us at any given time. In the case of the ref, she must choose which bits of data flooding her senses will receive her attention and which to ignore.

The coach yelling from the sideline, the outraged fan, the negative press from her last game, COVID-related game cancellations? *Ignore.* The ball in the cylinder, the jostling players, the three steps before putting the ball on the floor, the shot clock? *Focus.* For now, anyway.

Gorillas in Our Midst

Honestly, our distractibility has served us well. This inability to focus isn't the enemy. We are acting on an innate desire to seek information; behaviors that support the accumulation of information immediately engage us. This notion, known as *information foraging*,[30] is supported by findings that molecular and physiological mechanisms that originally developed in our brains to support foraging for food have shifted to including foraging for information.[31]

According to Adam Gazzaley and Larry D. Rosen, professors of neuroscience and psychology:

> Engaging in behaviors that are intended to maximize exposure and consumption of new information, but end up causing interference, may be thought of as optimal. And so, such behaviors may be reinforced despite their negative consequences in other domains of our lives. Since humans seem to exhibit an innate drive to forage for information in much the same way

that other animals are driven to forage for food, we need to consider how this "hunger" is now fed to an extreme degree by modern technological advances that deliver highly accessible information.[32]

In short, our brains treat the need to gather information in much the same way as our ancestors regarded the act of foraging for food. Today that information is even more readily, constantly accessible. Even for our ancestors, the need to be attentive to environmental cues—keeping an ear out for predators, scanning the terrain for quicksand, watching the dark clouds on the horizon—was a form of information foraging. It has simply evolved to a point where, for today's individual, information foraging is a primary physiological and psychological need. Unfortunately, we reinforce these behaviors, even when we know they aren't good for us.

The problem here is that there is simply too much information available, and we aren't very good at deciding what we attend to and what we discard. Here's an example:

As . . . you . . . carefully . . . read . . . each . . . and . . . every . . . word . . . of . . . this . . . sentence . . .

. . . your mind focuses on each one with clarity for a fraction of a second, dedicating a portion of your attention to your reading. Equally important to the information you take in is the parallel process of excluding other information that competes for that same attention. If your brain didn't have the capability to decide which sliver of the information bombarding your senses would become the target of your brain's processing power, you would be unable to take in everything that's in front of you.

This filtering ability, which enables us to determine which information gets our conscious attention—and thus is subject to analysis, comparison, and choice—and which takes a back seat is known as *selectivity*. The concept is simple: faced with a constant barrage of sensory overload, our brains must select which input to attend to and which to ignore in order to navigate the demands of daily life.

For example, imagine you are sitting with a loved one who is unloading to you about their horrible day at work. As the tears erupt, you look this person in the eye, recognizing that this is a time when you need to be fully present to give comforting reassurance. But just as you are about to speak words of solace—oh no! You remember you have a crucial appointment, and you'll be late if you don't start getting ready. Then the dog scratches at the door, your cell phone buzzes, and you knock over the water bottle in front of you. You think to yourself, *Focus!* It feels like your attention is gone.

Not quite. Attention can be diverted, but it never really vanishes, even though it may feel that way. Attention can become depleted, however. Think about lifting weights. When you're doing bicep curls, the first two or three might be relatively easy. But as you continue to curl, your muscles become fatigued, lifting the weight becomes more difficult, and eventually you reach what trainers call *failure*. The muscle is exhausted, and only after some rest can it exert more force. Attention operates according to a similar principle, if not the same physiology. When our attention is confronted with too many simultaneous demands, it becomes diluted and weakened, making it harder to engage where we intend or want. But attention never goes away.

Cognitive neuroscience explains this through the concept of *load theory*. Take, for example, a drive down the highway. As you begin your journey, you pull into a busy intersection before merging onto the highway on-ramp. Your attention is sharply focused on the green light, the merge, and the position of the cars in adjacent lanes. The demands—the "load"—for your attention are caused by the many actions and events occurring simultaneously around you. Your load is *high*. After you merge onto the highway, and the road begins to open up into an enjoyable ride, the competing demands for your attention decrease. With the lessened load, your cognitive resources are freed to focus on listening to your audiobook, thinking about the day, or simply enjoying the ride. When demands were high, and your attention was focused, however, the load required all your attentional resources to keep you safe.

Even when your mind wanders during a long drive, and your focus changes, you always use 100 percent of your attention.[33] The direction of your attention might shift, but the amount of attention remains constant. The question is:

Where does our attention shift to?[34]

Generally, we are not even aware when our attention has changed focus—at least, not while it's happening. As with many of our mental states, we only notice them in retrospect. We often don't notice when we disengage until we look back and rebuke ourselves for doing so. The irony is, even when we are able to attend to an important task in front of us, our attention can be too narrow or wide, too focused or unfocused. Attention is often a blunt instrument, and depending on where we focus it and with what intensity, we can become blinded to other areas that also deserve our attention.

This is known in cognitive psychology as *inattentional blindness*, demonstrated in well-known studies conducted by psychologists and researchers Christopher Chabris and Daniel Simons. In a famous demonstration, participants were shown a video of a group of people passing around a basketball. Participants were instructed to count the number of times three players wearing white shirts passed the ball. Thirty seconds into the video, a woman in a gorilla suit walks across the floor into the middle of the group, stops, faces the camera, and pounds her chest. She then walks away.

As participants were debriefed on the video, they provided a count of the passes made between those wearing white shirts. They were then asked, "But did you see the gorilla?" Half of the viewers had completely missed her. Many of them looked right at her and didn't see her—or more to the point, she didn't register consciously. Even after they were told about the gorilla, they were certain they hadn't missed the unexpected guest pounding her chest. Once they were shown the video without the attention cue, they were stunned to see the gorilla.

The video went viral and has appeared in countless psychology textbooks. It is featured at more than a dozen science museums as well as in the popular and academic press. It's been used by advertising agencies, television shows, preachers, corporate trainers, and even anti-terrorist units as an illustration of how focused attention in one area can make us oblivious to something else that, by all rights, should have us saying, "Wait, what?"

Missing the Obvious

In 2010 the researchers conducted a sequel to the study; however, because the video had become part of the popular culture, most viewers weren't falling for it. This time they were watching for the gorilla to make her entrance, and when she did they saw her. This time, however, they failed to notice other unexpected events, such as the curtain changing color in the background or some of the basketball passers walking out of the simulation.[35]

How is this possible? How can we miss what is right in front of us? How can a referee be blind to what we can see from our living-room armchair? Inattentional blindness highlights the limits of our eyes *and* our brains. When we focus our attention on a narrow subset of our environment—precisely the type of cognition that's required to engage in virtually any demanding task, from cooking a gourmet meal to writing this paragraph—we usually fail to notice other things around us. Unfortunately, that might well mean we miss what we really want to see or desperately need to notice.

To further illustrate this point, Chabris and Simons point to a 1995 incident in which police pursued four suspects leaving the scene of a shooting. One of the officers chased down a suspect on foot. Two other officers, arriving after the officer had begun pursuit, mistook the first officer for a suspect, and they began beating the first officer. At the same time, a fourth officer took up the pursuit of the original suspect, running past the beating that was taking place among the three officers.

When the matter was taken up in court, the fourth officer—the cop who ran past the men in blue laying a beat-down on their fellow officer—denied seeing the thrashing and was convicted of perjury and obstruction of justice. The conviction, the researchers said, "Raised an intriguing legal issue: Could an eyewitness actually fail to notice an assault like that one?" They put the convicted officer's alibi to the test.

In their experiment, the two researchers enlisted participants to run behind an assistant, counting the number of times he touched his hat. Part way into their run, the assistant, with participants in hot pursuit, ran past a staged fight in which two men appeared to be beating another man.

When debriefed postrun, more than 40 percent of the pursuers had missed the bogus fight, even in daylight. Sixty-five percent missed it when the experiment was repeated at night. Researchers determined that, in light of the experiment, it was possible the fourth officer had truly overlooked the beating of his comrade completely and that his testimony may well have been truthful.[36]

NERD ALERT!

We think hands-free phones are the no-harm, no-foul way to carry on conversations while driving, but that's not so. The rate of distracted-driving accidents involving those using hands-free phones is equal to that of drivers using handheld phones. Research by the American Automobile Association found that some tasks performed while driving required greater attention than others. Listening to the radio or casual conversation while driving don't consume a great deal of cognitive resources; however, talking on the phone or texting, even with aids such as verbal text-messaging apps or hands-free phone technology, demand significant amounts of our limited attention, engage a variety of our cognitive resources, and distract us from the road, even when we're looking straight ahead, and our hands are on the wheel.[37]

The Limits of Our Attention

Selectivity and inattentional blindness play an important role in culling the inexhaustible data bombarding our senses. That's vital for our practical function in the world, where we have to complete one mundane task after another. At the same time, we have a distorted understanding of the limits of our attention, and as illustrated by the invisible gorilla experiment and its follow-up research, most of us are dangerously unaware of those limits.

Think of the last time you drove home from work while talking on the hands-free phone in your car. Sure, you stopped at the three—or was it four?—red lights, but how much of that drive do you remember in detail? Did you arrive at your destination unaware of how much time had passed? Now think about another drive when you encountered something sudden and unexpected, like the driver in front of you locking up their brakes to avoid an obstacle in the road. In a fraction of a second, your attention switched from your phone call to the immediate need to hit the brakes or swerve to avoid a collision. When that happened, your attention instantly diverted away from your phone call, and it became background noise. Once the crisis was averted, and you were back on the road home unscathed, you had the luxury of turning your attention *back* to the call. Not only is our attention narrow in its focus but it is dynamic.

We can apply this same circumstance to the Swipe. Let's say you're an amateur painter making your latest attempt to complete a complex portrait, the most challenging thing you've ever tried to paint. When you're completely engaged in the work, the rest of the world seems to drop away. The act of painting—of the real-time calculus of brushstroke, color, and light—consumes all your attention. You might not even hear the phone ring or the dog whining to be let out, and if you stay in that state, you could paint for hours and then look up to realize with a start that it's nighttime.

But if the painting isn't going well, or if you're filled with self-doubt, you're not as bulletproof to the distractions around you. Your attention wanders off, comes back to the work, wanders again, and then you drag it back to the canvas, maybe even chiding yourself: "Focus!" If you're feeling discomfort over your ability to paint, or unsure of the quality of the work in front of you, on one of those occasions your attention goes off the rails, you'll follow it. You'll get up and let the dog out, and then clean up the kitchen, and then check your phone, and—you know the drill.

Distractions are a given because of how our brains filter stimuli. Swiping is an unconscious decision to allow those distractions to seduce our attention away from what's important and refocus it on what's trivial, all as a way of avoiding distressing emotions. Our distractibility is neither entirely physical nor visual, but an issue of attention.[38] Our minds are wandering nearly half the time we are awake—even when the stakes are high or the outcome of inattention could be dire. The issue is, do we allow them to continue wandering?

This is a critical question, because as Adam Sandler's distracted-father character in *Click*, the NBA referee, a driver on his cell phone, students pushing keyboard space bars, missile silo officers sleeping with their hands on the big red nuclear button, cops chasing down a suspect, and the parent talking to the child can all attest:

What we pay attention to becomes the life we experience.

Being Significant

Is being distracted the same thing as Swiping? No. We are neurologically and psychologically predisposed to distraction. Distractions will always be there, trying to pickpocket our attention. It's not distraction that robs us of life's moments; it's what we choose to do with our attention. The Swipe occurs when we hear the siren song of distraction and continually follow that song. It's a failure to understand what attention is and how to manage it. It's a product of the magical thinking that suggests attention, focus, and flow *just happen* instead of being the results of comprehensible neurological processes.

In the lyrics to his song "Beautiful Boy (Darling Boy)," John Lennon paraphrases American journalist Allen Saunders: "Life is what happens to us while we are making other plans."[39] What we Swipe to becomes our life for that moment in time. Whatever we pay attention to becomes amplified.[40] Logically, if we continually Swipe and spend our attention on relatively meaningless tasks, pop culture confections, and frivolous activities, those distractions become an ever more important piece of our lives. Is that really what we want?

The goal here is not to eliminate distraction from our lives. We couldn't even if we wanted to, because our brains are wired for distraction. What we can do is learn to understand the nature of distraction and attention, accept that attention is a limited resource, and develop the metacognition not only to watch our attention wax and wane in real time but to understand why it does so. Then we can begin to exercise control over how we spend what might be our most precious resource for creating the life we see when we close our eyes.

It's possible to do this. Ongoing cognitive studies[41] repeatedly show that when we are aware of where our attention is focused, we perform better.[42] We also know that when we become more aware of when our attention is drifting, we can catch ourselves mind-wandering and make the necessary course corrections before we become disengaged. The goal, then, is to be mindful of our attention, recognize when our distractions become Swipes, and steer our attention back to engaging in the reality—and life—we want to create.

CHAPTER 9

Master Your Attention

> When we focus our attention on a task and spend time repeating it, we take it off our mental whiteboard and reach the point where excellence becomes automatic: mastery. If the behavior we practice most often is Swiping, however, do we become masters of the Swipe?

If the gorilla video and distracted police officer who didn't see his partner being beaten up right in front of him reveal anything, it's the fragile, fleeting nature of our ability to sustain attention and engagement. Nevertheless, *your* ability to pay attention is probably top notch. You are a master of multitasking, right? Well, you may want to think that through, but put down your phone first.

The term *multitasking* is taken not from psychology, business, or even neuroscience. Multitasking comes from the tech world and refers to the ability of a system to do more than one thing at the same time. Neuroscientists and researchers Adam Gazzaley and

Larry Rosen describe the process of multitasking as processing simultaneous multiple operations.

In their book, *The Distracted Mind*, the researchers describe what differentiates computers with multitasking capabilities from those limited to single processing. According to their work, single-processing computers "end up doing something much more akin to what our brains do when we ask them to perform multiple operations at the same time." This is not true multitasking, in which all system resources are available to all applications. Instead, the system processor assumes the role of traffic cop, giving preference to some tasks and allocating less processing power to others. This is how our brains work when the tasks at hand require cognitive control. Our prefrontal cortex essentially serves as the traffic cop, switching between neural networks and deciding to which tasks the brain's limited resources should be directed.[1]

Many of us claim to be more productive when we multitask. It's convenient to fire off a couple of emails while sitting in on a business call. Checking for text messages during a class lecture means a student can both listen to the lecture and make plans for the evening. Telephone calls are great because we can simultaneously take the call, send an email, message three coworkers, surf the internet, and check the performance of our portfolio. We get more done in the same amount of time, right?

Stanford professors Cliff Nass and colleagues conducted three studies to evaluate just how true this is. First, the researchers sent a survey to potential subjects and broke them down into two groups based on their responses: high multitaskers, who routinely navigated multiple forms of media simultaneously—cell phone, internet, television, social media—and low multitaskers, who did not. Study participants were grouped and then tested for their multitasking aptitude, or lack thereof.

First, they were tested for their ability to ignore irrelevant or distracting information. On a screen in front of the participants flashed two red rectangles and either two, four, six, or zero blue rectangles. When the screen was shown again, participants were asked to determine whether one of the red rectangles had been rotated. As the researchers added more rectangles to the image, the high multitaskers got worse and worse at determining whether the red rectangles had shifted. Low multitaskers were consistently more accurate, regardless of the number of distracting blue rectangles. High multitaskers were poor at ignoring irrelevant information— the addition of blue rectangles.

In the next round, participants were tested on their ability to organize information. They were presented with a string of letters, which they were required to keep track of: *L, Y, T, M, Q, A, M—stop!*

They were instructed to press a button when they saw a letter they had already seen three letters previously. In this case, the letter *M* had occurred three letters prior to the second occurrence. Again, high multitaskers performed far worse at this task than did low multitaskers. Not only were the high multitaskers repeatedly scoring worse than low multitaskers but this poor performance also appeared to worsen over time.

Finally, the team tested the participants' skill in switching tasks midstream. Screens flashed two options: "letter" and "number." They were then shown a letter-number combination, such as A7 or J4. If the prior screen flashed "number," they were asked to determine whether the letter-number pair was odd or even (A7 = odd; J4 = even). If the screen flashed "letter," participants would indicate whether the letter in the pair was a vowel or a consonant

(A7 = vowel; J4 = consonant). After a series of "number" tasks, the screens switched to "letter" tasks. As with previous trials, high multitaskers significantly underperformed when compared to their low multitasking counterparts.

"The shocking discovery of this research is that [high multi-taskers] are lousy at everything that's necessary for multitasking," Nass concluded. "The irony here is that when you ask the low multitaskers, they all think they're much worse at multitasking and the high multitaskers think they're gifted at it."[2]

NERD ALERT!

Congratulations! Your attention span is now less than that of a goldfish! The attention of the beloved bowl dweller is about nine seconds, but now, according to a Microsoft study, people lose attention at about the eight-second mark. A survey of 2,000 participants, as well as a study of brain activity (EEGs) of 112 others, found that since the year 2000, the average attention span has dropped from twelve seconds to eight seconds.[3] Take that, goldfish! We're number one! We're number one! We're number . . . what were we saying?

Multitasking or Task Switching?

Is multitasking a real thing? Psychology and neurology textbooks tell us it's ineffective, even that it's impossible. Yet anyone strolling down a busy city street might spot a fellow pedestrian walking briskly while texting, eating a veggie wrap, glancing up at stoplights, and listening to music on their AirPods on the way to their destination. How is this possible?

A Washington State University study looked at alleged multitasking and how it affected studying. It found that the most frequent activities students were involved in while studying were listening to music, texting, and social media, as any student or parent could tell you. The researchers found that students who texted or used social media while studying reported that their mobile phone use interfered significantly with their studying. Meanwhile, those who listened to music did not experience the same distractions.

If you immediately noticed that the passive activity, which didn't require conscious engagement, was less intrusive, give yourself a gold star. The findings indicated that "the difference between the effects of passive listening to music and active engagement in testing or social media highlights a major intrusion in media in everyday life. Traditional media, such as radio, television, or music, which can be ignored as background noise, are fundamentally different from human interactions via text message or social media."[4]

So, yes, multitasking is possible, and it is constantly occurring within our daily lives. But *true* multitasking is only possible when two conditions are met. First, at least one of the tasks must be "automatic," meaning it does not require conscious attention or higher-order cognitive processing. The example of people walking down the city streets while eating and listening to music is accurate because we can engage in those actions without thinking about them.

Second, the tasks must involve different types of brain processing, such as listening to music while studying. Music and studying involve different parts of the brain. But your ability to retain information from your studies while listening to the new lyrics of an unfamiliar song will be significantly reduced, as both studying and processing lyrics activate the language center of the brain.

In other words, the brain can perform only one conscious process at a time. Lower-order processing does not require attention. Listening to music, walking, or eating don't generally require conscious thought—these processes are "automatic" System One activities. As stated by Gazzaley and Rosen: "Our brains do not parallel process information, as demanded by many of our daily activities, if those activities require cognitive control. This failure of our brain to truly multitask at a neural level represents a major limitation in our ability to manage our goals."[5]

So here's the reality of our multitasking claims:

Most of what we call "multitasking" is actually "task switching."

Task switching is what occurs when we attempt to talk on the phone and respond to an email at the same time, or drive and talk while on a hands-free phone. While the hands-free device eliminates the physical distraction of holding a phone to your ear, it requires cognitive attentional engagement. As a result, we rapidly switch back and forth between these tasks, even if it is not our intention to do so, and even if we are not aware we are switching. This is why we often see drivers driving slowly or erratically when speaking on their phones. This is why, if you're trying to take a call and answer an email, you end up waiting until the other person is speaking to turn your attention to your computer, write a sentence of your email reply, then turn your attention back to the call and inevitably say, "I'm so sorry. I missed what you just said. Could you repeat that?"

It turns out we really do have one-track minds.

When we engage in multiple activities that compete for conscious cognitive resources, our brains must switch between the tasks. Findings by the American Psychological Association demonstrate that this shift is neither fast nor smooth; there is a lag during which your brain must recalibrate to the new task. Although the transition may feel instantaneous, it takes time—up to 40 percent longer than single tasking. Complex tasks may take up to 40 percent longer to complete multiple tasks than a single task.[6] Even simple distractions can require tenths of a second.[7]

The irony is that the worst task switchers appear to be unaware of the impact this has on their ability to accomplish goals. First, we are often oblivious to the amount of time we spend on the distracting task, typically underestimating the time it takes to attend to the distraction. When the distraction is technology, we are also naive about the amount of time we end up spending on the distracting text. We also greatly underestimate the additional follow-up tasks that result from responding to the secondary task, all of which prevent us from getting back to the original task.

Even more time consuming and potentially damaging, perhaps, is the cognitive rabbit hole distractions can lead us down. More than one vacation has gone south when someone said, "I'll just check my email—it will only take a minute," only to find that after they put down the mobile device their thoughts for the next three hours were consumed with the content of the email rather than the gorgeous ocean vista they went there to see. Getting lost in the minutiae of trivial tasks and technology-mediated faux experiences pulls our attention away from being in the moment with the people we love, and from life's peak experiences.

Task switching is a problem limited to Generation Z, right? Well, not so much. It turns out we're all guilty of short attention span syndrome. A Time Inc. study observed groups of younger and older adults. Participants wore biometric belts with embedded eyeglass cameras for three hundred hours. The study found that younger adults switched tasks an average of every two minutes. Older adults weren't much better, switching tasks every three to four minutes.[8]

The Whiteboard

For more, we turn to neuropsychology—specifically, what cognitive psychologists refer to as *working memory*—blended with a touch of computer science.

Think of how data is handled and stored on any computer—your phone, your laptop, etc. Random-access memory (RAM) acts as a short-term space for storing data that must be accessed quickly and on a short-term basis. RAM allows your laptop to handle ongoing tasks, such as surfing the internet, writing the most recent chapter of your novel, or finishing that mission in *Halo Infinite*. RAM allows for switching between tasks and swapping between multiple applications. It's considered "volatile memory," or "temporary memory," meaning that all data is lost when the laptop loses power. In comparison, your computer's hard drive is considered "permanent," or "nonvolatile," storage. It stores data for the long term and retains that data even when the system is powered down.

The brain is orders of magnitude more complex than an Apple MacBook Pro, but the analogy works. Working memory, like RAM, is information that is held in the mind for short periods of time, allowing us to execute immediate cognitive tasks. This information could be abstract—an idea, a possibility—or concrete, such as counting car stalls in a parking lot. Suppose your friend told you, "Look for a blue Honda parked in the second lot to the east of the main administration building." To find the car, you would need to remember

- that the car was the object of the search;
- that the description provided the location of a car you were searching for;
- that finding the car was desirable;
- the location and appearance of the administration building;
- the meaning of *east*;
- the meaning of *blue*;
- the meaning of *second*; and
- how to distinguish a Honda automobile from other automobiles.

Of course, all these disparate operations of working memory seem instantaneous and automatic, so you don't think about them. But if you're programming a computer to perform the same function, you need to write code for each one. Once you get to the parking lot, all these pieces in your working memory would need to be pieced together in the right order and context in order to locate the vehicle.[9]

Cognitive psychologists often compare the temporary scratch space of working memory to a whiteboard, similar to what you might find in an office or a classroom. On that whiteboard we can jot down lists, draw pictures, lay out patterns and relationships, or throw out options to consider before making a decision.

But there's a difference between the scrawl on that whiteboard and the information we hold in working memory. While the ink on the whiteboard often proves stubbornly difficult to erase completely, the ink in our working memory begins to fade once we move on to another task, sometimes lasting only a few seconds. The only way to keep the ink fresh is to continue the same task. Working memory goes hand in hand with attention. If we want to keep important content on the board, vivid and visible, we must fix our attention on the task at hand.

What else is true of the whiteboards we use in our conference rooms? They get *messy*. When we're brainstorming and jumping from one idea to the next—exactly what occurs in task switching—the writing on the board can become confusing, even illegible. This also happens in our minds, and physical strain, such as stress and sleep deprivation, make the problem worse. But even without these complications, in the normal course of a day, our mental whiteboards become full. We have all had the sense that in order to think straight we need to "clear our minds." But the reality is, we can never completely clear our whiteboards. There is always something there. We immediately replace what we erase with something else. That's what the mind does. It thinks.

A key difference between our working memory and the whiteboard is that our working memory also contains, and can even be filled by, *emotion*. In this space, we recall past events and associate emotions with those events. This is where we construct the meaning of our experiences.

If an item is on the whiteboard, it becomes your experience, at least for that moment.[10]

Mastery

Psychology, neuropsychology, and brain science collaborate to turn these systems into performance, and nowhere is the potential of this combination clearer than in the performance of the elite athlete. How is it that elite athletes appear to be able to process an exhausting oversupply of sensory input simultaneously? Consider a Major League hitter at the plate, facing a pitcher throwing a one-hundred-mile-per-hour fastball. In the 375 to 400 milliseconds it takes that ball to cross the plate, the batter has to observe the pitcher's release point; see the ball's spin; take in the positioning of the fielders, the count, and the situation; see the pitch's location; and decide whether or not to swing. It's crazy that anyone can hit the ball at all, much less hit .300.

This exceptional ability isn't limited to so-called "fast-twitch" athletes. Endurance athletes exhibit a different type of exceptional performance. We've already broken down the limits of our attention and focus, so how does an endurance athlete run an Ironman triathlon or an extreme race—like the Leadville 100, a one-hundred-mile run that climbs to more than twelve thousand feet above sea level—while maintaining the focus and concentration necessary to keep going through exhaustion and agony? Like the elite baseball or football player, they're wired differently.

Simply put, top athletes are capable of feats that defy the capacity of the average person. An elite soccer player might field a pass from the goalie, dribble the ball downfield while sidestepping opponents, position the ball in front of the opposite foot, and kick the ball into the net with perfect finesse. But how? How are they able to multitask, when neuroscience tells us that when we do we're really not very good at it? Their performance seems automatic, running down the field on autopilot. In a sense, they *are* on autopilot.

A concept or idea begins in working memory. Over time, as the idea appears on our whiteboard more frequently, and we pay more attention to it, we "learn" it. Once it is learned, it becomes a part of long-term memory. Long-term memory is made up of the vast amount of information processed and saved over an individual's lifetime. Those ideas may be incomplete, or even inaccurate, but as our working memory continues to gather input, they are corrected and refined in long-term memory.

Anyone who has become adept at a task or series of tasks—playing the piano, refereeing a basketball game, running a triathlon, etc.—achieves a form of what is known as *mastery*. At the level of mastery, each step of a complex task no longer needs to be scribbled on the whiteboard. Instead, carrying out the task is part of an individual's *procedural memory*—a type of implicit memory. *Implicit memory* is unconscious, meaning we are not aware when it is used. Implicit memory works alongside its counterpart, *explicit memory*, which we access when we intentionally recall information, to form our long-term memory. Athletes, musicians, and other elite performers develop their impressive abilities over extensive periods of practice and experience. In fact, we all develop skills in various areas through repetition.

Through sufficient training, repetition, and practice, we experience *procedural learning*, in which we repeatedly engage in an activity until the necessary neural pathways begin working together to automatically produce the desired outcome without our conscious attention. When that occurs, we "master" an action. How is it that the NBA referee is able to focus so clearly on the call rather than the distractions? How does the seasoned marathoner hit mile twenty-four without thinking, *left foot, right foot,* or the experienced saxophone player slide effortlessly into the Paul

Desmond sax solo from "Take Five"? It's not conscious effort. It's procedural memory.

People who achieve mastery build up a huge storehouse of procedural memories. These are not conscious "play this key, then that key" memories, but are instead based on the ingrained memories of past experience and practice. Studies with athletes have shown that this memory isn't limited to muscles and movement. They also store things like the movement of a baseball, football, or golf ball through the air, or the relationship between the way the opponent's racquet swings and the likely trajectory of the ball as it leaves the strings.

The brain uses these memories to anticipate outcomes and make predictions. The more practice and repetition, the more accurate the predictions. At the highest levels, the greatest elite athletes can accurately predict where the ball and other players will be within a fraction of a second.[11] This is why some players seem to "see the whole game" in a way that lesser athletes cannot.

Are elite athletes generally mentally sharper than the rest of us when it comes to their chosen vocation? Studies seem to say, "Yes. Maybe." But does this mental acuity apply outside their sport? Depends which cognitive abilities we're talking about. Researchers and coaches experimented with tennis players and found them to be better than nonplayers at judging the differences in the speed of dots moving toward them. When tasked with identifying tennis balls in a visual scene, however, they performed no better than nonplayers, unless the scene was in the context of a tennis match.[12]

When asked to spot tennis balls in a game situation outside tennis—a cricket field, for example—tennis players performed no better than nonplayers. While their cognitive abilities were superior on the tennis court, they were dependent on the environment.

Another famous study looked at the brains of taxicab drivers and the effect of ongoing practice on their brains. To become a London cabbie, you must master "the Knowledge"—basically, memorizing the location and progress of every street, courtyard, square, hotel, Underground station, and other landmark in the vast city. It takes years. In the study, researchers compared the brains of London cab drivers to those of London bus drivers. Both drove within the same city, maneuvered through the same streets, and experienced similar levels of stress associated with big-city driving. But those driving buses stuck to constrained routes, with little or no deviation.

The study found that in the cabbies the posterior portion of the hippocampus—the area of the brain that handles spatial memory—had more gray matter—was bigger—than did the same region in the bus drivers. This area became larger the longer these cabbies were in their jobs. The conclusion: practice actually changes the physical structure of our brain.[13]

Another study looked at the brains of novice, expert, and elite archers. When involved in archery simulations, the brains of the novices showed widespread brain activity, especially in regions related to planning. In contrast, the brains of expert archers showed reduced activity in these areas when undergoing the same simulation. The experts appeared to be relying less on the frontal areas of the brain and more on specialized processing areas of the brain. This may be what makes it possible for experts to make decisions more quickly, efficiently, and using less energy than their less experienced counterparts.[14] System One, which conserves energy, handles the bulk of the processing before System Two is called upon.

In his 2005 book *Blink*, Malcolm Gladwell discusses the notion that much of our thinking goes on without thinking. Through the process he calls "thin-slicing," we make quick decisions based on only a tiny bit of information. It's likely you've heard of the "ten-thousand-hour rule," which became famous in Gladwell's 2008 book *Outliers*. The rule suggests that it takes ten thousand hours of intensive practice to achieve mastery in anything complex, becoming elite at a sport, playing the violin, and so on.

Gladwell's claim has been questioned by some. Generally speaking, practice is an unquestionable part of mastery; however, some researchers claim that practice accounts for about one-quarter of the overall effect.[15] Other factors, such as genetics, environment, teachers or coaches, enjoyment, reward, and individual motivation are also significant determinants as to whether someone reaches mastery. With the athlete, the effects of practice are visible in muscle tone, agility, strength, and speed. But the many hours on the field not only affect the bodies but the brains of athletes.

So it is with the rest of us. Practice and repetition aren't the only factors that determine if we master something, but they play a significant role. We become good at what we practice. More important, we become *what* we practice.

NERD ALERT!

Plato, Socrates, and Aristotle voiced their frustration with the concept of akrasia, which comes from the Greeks, meaning to act against one's better judgment, to self-indulge, or to lack command of oneself. They disagreed as to whether people don't do what is best for them because they lack self-control or because they make poor choices, but the philosophy giants agreed that akrasia prevents us from achieving our potential.

Swipe: The Anti-Master

Pretty simple, right? We get good at what we practice. We don't become good at what we don't. Therein lies the problem.

The first time we try anything, we're not good at it. It's hard. It's embarrassing. Practicing scales on the piano is mind-numbing drudgery; however, the more we practice, the clearer and stronger the associated neuropathways become. The task becomes easier and requires less effort. We're able to do it faster and easier, to the point that we begin working on autopilot. Our results become exponentially better. As a quote often attributed to Ralph Waldo Emerson says, "That which we persist in doing becomes easier for us to do—not that the nature of the thing has changed, but that our power to do is increased."

Interestingly, reintroducing conscious attention to something that you're able to do on autopilot actually decreases proficiency. If you've ever overthought a guitar lick, a golf shot, or even something as basic as walking down a flight of stairs, you know how interfering with this unconscious process actually worsens your performance of the task.

The typical human brain continues to develop until around the age twenty-five or twenty-six; however, our brains change throughout our lives. The brain's intriguing ability to form or reorganize new synaptic connections is known as *neuroplasticity*. Through experience and practice, we continue to strengthen these varying connections between neurons, while other connections wither away.[16]

This has big implications on our ability to achieve mastery, and for the hazards of the Swipe. It's reasonable to assume that when we engage in an activity with the intention of remaining engaged over a long period of time our goal is to achieve a level of mastery that corresponds to our natural ability. We may not all become J. K. Rowling or Yo-Yo Ma, but we aspire to reach our highest potential.

The trouble is, mastery depends on remaining engaged in the same task, job, relationship, or pursuit for an extended period of time. The Swipe makes that impossible. Remember that what's on our whiteboards—what's in our working memory—quickly fades. It must be refreshed if it is to stick. What constantly occupies our precious, limited whiteboard space? That whiteboard becomes our experience for that particular moment. Even if you are sitting on a park bench with your child, if your mind is ruminating about something you need to do at work, *you are at work*. Your mental activity creates your present experience.

Finally, whatever continually fills our whiteboard gets transferred to our long-term memory. If it's not on the whiteboard, or if it fades without being refreshed with new activity, it doesn't stay there long enough to make the jump to procedural memory. That means anything we don't spend extended time and conscious attention on doesn't become automatic. In other words:

When we Swipe continually, we have no hope of achieving mastery. We never really get good at anything, no matter how badly we want to.

The terrible irony of all this is that the innate abilities of our brains can be overridden, within reason, by intense practice and hard work. Yes, natural gifts matter, but even if endless practice and expert coaching can't make you Tiger Woods, you can reach the autopilot level and become an admirable golfer. Practice really does make perfect. You can achieve mastery, where something becomes easy and even supercharged.

If your response to difficulty and challenge is to Swipe, however, it's the Swipe itself that becomes automated, ingrained, and irresistible. In Swiping away from a focused, hard, demanding activity to a distraction, you're landing at a temporary destination, not something worth your attention. When you Swipe away from a tough workout, for instance, you're generally not shifting your attention to some other long-sought goal, such as becoming an expert woodworker or practicing the piano. You're shifting your attention to trivia—checking your phone, feeding your fish, making lunch, calling a friend. Instead of pursuing mastery, you're wasting time.

This means the only thing that sticks—the only neurological pattern that eventually becomes part of your procedural memory—is the pattern that leads you to Swipe, the pattern that makes you flee in panic from a desirable task that tests your capacity in order to avoid confronting your temporary distress or doubt. In other words, if you Swipe long enough and often enough, turning away from the challenges that speak to your deepest values, you will eventually *master the Swipe*.

Swiping will be what you're good at.

All you're good at.

Why can't you ever finish what you start? This is why.

Now let's see what we can do to change that.

CHAPTER 10

Escaping the Hamster Wheel

The Hamster Wheel is only part of the Swipe story. Past the Crossroads, there's another path—another part of the wheel. If we can become aware of the precursors of Swiping—the emotional and psychological warning signs that we're about to rationalize, diminish, or surrender—then we can turn reflexive panic into intentional decision to persist, adapt, and actually finish what we start. We master our attention and defeat the Swipe.

Aviad Faruz, founder of online jewelry retailer Faruzo, has given a lot of thought to why people tend not to finish what they start, even when that pursuit means a great deal to them. "As a founder, I can say that thinking about the end goal and the prize I'll get for doing a thing or project is the main reason why I start," he said in an email, "and it's the same for others. People tend to pursue things because they want something to happen, which is only possible if they've finished what they started."

"However, there are times that while in the middle of something we lose our interest and feel that we don't want it anymore, or maybe we still want it but not that much," he continues. "I think that's because we lack connection with the goal that we want to achieve. It's probable that we were just overwhelmed by the idea of something at the start, but that excitement gradually fades because we didn't really want it that much. Our desires and reasons are insufficient to keep us going."

Faruz is onto something. While motivation and a sense of purpose (the "meaning" in MAGIC) factor into our ability to achieve a goal after it becomes challenging, they are rarely sufficient on their own to get us across the finish line. Look at the millions who try to quit smoking each year. It's safe to say that the majority of those individuals really *want* to stop smoking and be healthier. Yet that desire isn't enough to overcome their habitual behavior patterns or the physical addiction to nicotine. Wanting something badly is what's known in screenwriting as the *inciting incident*, the event that breaks the main character out of normalcy and starts them on a new path. But it's insufficient to propel us all the way down that unknown road to the finish line.

The ultimate goal here is not to reach the Crossroads and then choose not to Swipe. It's to not entertain the idea of Swiping at all—to bypass that critical junction altogether. Sounds nice, but desire alone doesn't short-circuit the neural pathways that lead from the exultation of the Downhill to the outrage and surrender of the Uphill. Wanting something won't ever be enough to stop us from rationalizing failure in order to make it okay to duck discomfort.

We'll just make the usual promise—"It will be different next time"—and merrily Swipe away weeks or months of effort.

Not Swiping means understanding there's another part to the Hamster Wheel we talked about back in chapter 6—the part many of us don't know about, the part that, if we can access it, can free us from the endless cycle of "aspire, strive, quit, regret, repeat." What would happen if we followed the harder but more satisfying road instead of Swiping? We would bypass the Crossroads completely and instead follow a new path marked by the following mileposts:

1. Recognize and Reflect
2. Accept (and Appreciate) Discomfort
3. Adapt and Adjust
4. Reflect, Again and Again
5. Complete Something
6. Repeat

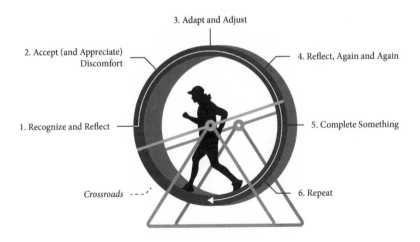

1. Recognize and Reflect

According to organizational psychologist Dr. Tasha Eurich, when we see ourselves and our performance clearly, we are more confident, more creative, and better performers. Yet, while 95 percent of us believe we are self-aware, only 10 to 15 percent actually are. But deep reflection isn't always beneficial. Rumination and reexamining everything about our pasts, says Eurich, can be counterproductive. Her research found that people who spent a lot of time in self-reflection were not only less self-aware than those who were not reflective, but also more anxious, less satisfied with their lives, and less happy.[1]

Exhaustive self-examination, however, is not the kind of reflection we're talking about here. Instead, taking a detour off the Hamster Wheel and onto the path of accomplishing what you set out to do means real-time reflection and self-awareness in the moment when the difficulty or discomfort of something becomes overwhelming. In that pivotal moment, when you're tempted to Swipe out of sheer panic, you stop yourself from reacting, take a minute, and think about what you're feeling and why.

Are your emotions justified? How are they showing up physically in your body? Are you allowing your attention to be pulled to something trivial as a defense mechanism? Are you on the verge of reacting to something real, or are you reacting to your fear? By reflecting in that moment, you're slowing things down—giving your prefrontal cortex, the reasoning part of your brain, time to override the amygdala, the part of your brain that governs your fight-or-flight response. You're putting you back in the driver's seat.

This is not an easy thing to do. Stephen Covey, the author of the classic *The Seven Habits of Highly Effective People*, wrote: "Between stimulus and response there is a space. In that space is our power to choose our response. In our response lies our growth and our freedom."[2] That idea—which was not original to Covey, and which is often incorrectly attributed to Austrian psychologist and Holocaust survivor Viktor Frankl—might be one of the most powerful insights in all self-improvement literature or psychology, but that doesn't mean it's easy to apply.

As an example, let's take an experience common to just about anyone who has learned to scuba dive: spitting the regulator. You're underwater in a pool or the shallows of the ocean, wearing your scuba gear, perhaps practicing clearing water out of your mask, when suddenly your mouthpiece comes loose, and your regulator pops out of your mouth. Instead of getting a lungful of air, you suck in water. Instantly, you panic and kick for the surface. That's not a failure of courage; that's biology! That's your fight-or-flight center telling you, "Breathe! Now!" because as far as it knows, if you don't get oxygen immediately, you'll die.

The first time you lose your regulator, that's what happens. Maybe the second time too. But the third time, you respond differently. The next time you lose your regulator, you begin to panic, but this time you catch yourself. Your self-aware mind interrupts your panic response and you think, *Wait a second. I'm not going to drown. I need to stay calm and find my regulator.* You reach around you with your hands, locate your regulator, pop it back in your mouth, clear it, take a breath, and you're fine. Just like that, you've overcome your panic. You'll probably never have that response again.

In order to not succumb to panic, however, you must first realize you are about to do just that, or that you're already in the grip of alarm. Divers and pilots, to cite two examples, learn to recognize that panic state in themselves and in others. Note that the key is *not* that you *don't* panic. Your ingrained biological response to discomfort or fear is still there. But by recognizing and reflecting, you defuse it. You rob it of its power to control your actions.

When you confront page fifty-one of a book manuscript or the second month of P90X, and you run into a wall of self-doubt or embarrassment, you'll still be tempted to say, "I can't do this. I quit!" In that space between stimulus and response, you reflect on what you've learned in this book, and what you've learned about yourself. You question your impulse to succumb to distraction or quit before the finish line. *Wait a second—I'm about to Swipe!* What's provoking it? Is it something real? What's at stake? You might ask:

- "Is Swiping my knee-jerk reaction to this situation, and am I about to Swipe?"
- "How did I get here? What were the precursors?"
- "Am I falling victim to past patterns? Is it time to interrupt or change them?"
- "In persisting and not Swiping, will I be doing more to honor the values—that which I hold to be of greater worth—that are important to me than I will by Swiping?"
- "How have my past failures to finish impacted my sense of self-worth, and how might making it to the finish line this time improve my self-worth?"
- "What am I Swiping to?"
- "Who am I if I continue to Swipe, versus who I could become if I can see this through to the end? Could finishing be a new beginning?"

These are not easy questions. They're also not the only way to explore patterns, values, self-worth, and identity. You may come up with others; however, change must begin somewhere, and it's hard to think of a better place than at that pivotal moment when you gather the strength and self-awareness to confront that moment of panic and say, "Not this time."

NERD ALERT!

As you try to stop Swiping, you won't simply engage in Reflection once and then everything's all good. During the pursuit of a single goal, such as succeeding at work, training for a race, or keeping a marriage together, you will face many, many moments in which you're tempted to Swipe, and each of them will demand that you stop, reflect, and make a conscious choice how to proceed. Yes, that seems exhausting, but did you really expect anything else? In any difficult pursuit, there are always successive setbacks and new challenges to come. The good news is, not Swiping gets easier. Under the psychological principle of *habituation*, your response to a stimulus decreases the more you're exposed to it. That's why you panic the first time you lose your scuba regulator, but not the third time. Your body has learned not to overreact. So the more you encounter Crossroads moments and have to stop and reflect, the easier it will become to do so. Eventually, you won't be tempted to Swipe at all. Trust us on this.

2. Accept (and Appreciate) Discomfort

When you reflect on your options and decide not to Swipe, you're also choosing to accept the discomfort you're feeling. It might be the sense that you don't have the talent to achieve something, that you're wasting your time trying to lose weight, that you're going to humiliate yourself, literal physical discomfort involved in working out or training for a race, boredom or temporary disengagement, or any one of a dozen other unpleasant, distressing sensations.

Regardless of the nature of the discomfort, at this point you make an immense cognitive shift. Instead of fleeing from potential pain, you choose to confront it. You defy Freud's pleasure principle and accept the idea that, just maybe, that pain won't be as great as your fear has made it out to be, and that you might benefit from it. That's a huge step.

Uncomfortable experiences are essential to our personal and professional growth. Only when we are exposed to conditions that force us to stretch our capacities and try new things do we discover the truth about our character, talents, and work ethic. Choosing to embrace and even appreciate discomfort rather than run from it is not only the key to moving past the Swipe; it's also a life-affirming, empowering act of intentionality. We choose to change our pattern of quitting and surrender. We make the statement that discomfort and inconvenience are not the end of our aspirations, but mere bumps in the road.

Australian clinical psychologist Leanne Hall expresses this idea beautifully. "By acknowledging discomfort and seeing it as an opportunity for growth we can move through it, instead of going around it," she writes. "Not only is this more likely to take us in the direction of our goals, it also teaches us amazing things about what our mind and body can achieve along the way. It provides us with an opportunity to get to know ourselves better both physically and psychologically. And when we know ourselves better, our lives become richer. We are better at setting healthy boundaries, better at understanding our limits, and better at supporting others."[3]

3. Adapt and Adjust

In psychology, adaptation is the ability to adjust to new information and experiences. Learning comes as a result of adapting to the changing environment. Through adaptation, we adopt new behaviors that make it possible for us to cope with change. We adjust to the requirements for success.

Once you've made the choice to lean into hardship and doubt, you can't keep doing things the same way. In this next stage on the wheel, it's time to adapt and adjust. You can't keep doing things the way you have been, because that's what led to the slow progress or painful stumbles that made you vulnerable to distraction and tempted you to Swipe in the first place. For example, let's say that for years you've pursued the goal of starting your own business. Over and over, you write business plans, talk to investors, design logos, and even rent office space. This new adventure has been thought out, designed, planned, talked about, and anticipated. But for some reason you can't ever make the leap. Something's stopping you, and after years of failure you realize it's the fear of leaving your full-time job. After all, it's a great job, and you thoroughly enjoy the team you work with. But you know it's not your future, and you have limited opportunity for growth. Still, you worry that you won't make enough money in your business to pay your bills and will lose your house, among the other unlikely disasters your overheated brain conjures up.

Eventually, you gain enough insight into your own mind to understand that if you keep letting this fear control you, you'll never start your company. You will stay and stagnate. But you make the choice to move past the anxiety, to live with it and not let it stop you. Bravo! But how will you change the course of events? How will you ensure that things turn out differently than the other six times you've sworn, "This is the year I take the leap"? You adapt. You change the game. You leave your job, giving yourself no choice: sink or swim. And that road less traveled makes all the difference.

What about those of us who aren't entrepreneurs? Perhaps through introspection and research you come to realize that an entrepreneurial lifestyle isn't for you. But you've disengaged from your current role, and your discomfort with a new assignment has caused you to circulate your résumé in the job market. Then, by asking yourself tough questions, you see that the problem isn't the job; it's your approach to the work. You decide that, rather than eschewing the difficult assignment that has you feeling extreme stress, you will lean into it, treating it as an opportunity to stretch—and, perhaps, even move to the next level personally and professionally. Yes, there are a few things about the assignment that don't work for you, others that you don't agree with, and a few that simply need to be adjusted, but you choose to accept that. You hold off on the job hunt and resolve instead to adjust what you can and adapt to what you can't.

A client of ours, Karina, was in this spot several years ago. As the head of design for a large, well-known marketing agency, she had worked for the firm for several years, when the company announced significant changes. Karina questioned both the direction of the company and her role. Her immediate reaction was to say, "I'm out of here!" But after spending some time talking it through with her, we identified what was really going on.

Karina saw that her pending resignation was an emotional Swipe caused by the insecurity over where she might fit into the new company structure. So, rather than disengage, she adapted to the change, rolled with it, and eventually discovered that the new organizational direction provided unanticipated opportunities for her to grow in what might have otherwise become a stagnant career. The challenges she faced as she adapted to her new world prepared her for her current role; three years later, Karina became the company's first female CEO in its forty-year existence. Even more impressive, the company's revenue increased by nearly 30 percent in her first year at the helm.

Daniel Hess, a writer-filmmaker from Baltimore, understands the necessity of adaptation. "For a long time, I suffered from not finishing creative projects or seeing them through completely," he wrote in our interview. "Personally, it was a matter of just feeling overwhelmed and then giving up when it all didn't come to life at once. As I've gotten older, though, I've found a great trick: taking things piece by piece. Like building a house, brick by brick. Since I've been able to use these skills, the number of projects I have managed to finish has been amazing."

Adaptations can be relatively trivial, or they can be momentous. The absolute degree of adaptation is less important than the *delta*— the degree of change over the previous state, the Swiping state. Your level of commitment also factors into the equation. A strong mental and emotional commitment to a small adaptation is preferable to a commitment to a major adaptation that you abandon the moment things go sideways. A novice author who's never completed a book might alter the entire trajectory of her writing career by vowing to write one thousand words per day, rain or shine. That may not seem like much, but in sixty days she could have a completed manuscript. That's the power of small adaptations.

The key to adapting under these circumstances is that adaptations are *voluntary* and *intentional*. They're not emergency reactions to adverse conditions—adapt or die. As a part of the spectrum of behaviors that begins with electing to accept discomfort, you're also making the call to adapt preemptively as a strategy for success instead of adapting involuntarily as a response to bitter failure. You choose to make changes in your daily routine, workspace, or associations in order to eliminate the distractions that pull your attention away from your work. When you adapt as a way to overcome limiting factors that are part of your personality, you're showing the foresight and honest self-evaluation that many people never manage. This is a big step forward.

4. Reflect, Again and Again

In his novel *Kafka on the Shore*, Haruki Murakami writes: "Once the storm is over, you won't remember how you made it through, how you managed to survive. You won't even be sure, whether the storm is really over. But one thing is certain. When you come out of the storm, you won't be the same person who walked in. That's what this storm's all about."[4]

That's the real message of this alternate path, but what a lot of people don't realize is that the storms keep coming, one after the other, until you reach the end of your journey. You won't hit one decision point where you're tempted to Swipe; you're going to hit many of them. At each one, you'll have to go through the same process of reflection and conscious choice.

This is normal. There is no smooth, trouble-free glide path to completing something you've never done before, or something that pushes your capabilities to their limit. You'll have to deal with poor performance, exhaustion and burnout, bewilderment, self-doubt, time crunches—the entire spectrum of Swipe-inducing frustrations—and with each you'll be tempted yet again to surrender to distractions and give up, even engaging in that momentary self-delusion: "I'll come back to it, and it will be better."

At each Crossroads, you'll face the same challenge—to catch yourself while the impulse to quit and *run* is tickling your adrenal glands and to calmly say, "Let's everybody take a moment." To apply your rational cognition—your mindfulness, self-awareness, and perspective—so you can disable the fight-or-flight instinct before it goes too far. Each time you reach that point, you'll have to talk yourself down from the ledge, so to speak, so you can keep making progress toward your Want. If you're engaged in something new that plays out over a period of months, you might encounter this moment of stress and choice twenty times or more, especially after a rough day or a questionable outcome.

Hal Gregersen, MIT professor, author, and executive director of MIT's Leadership Center, states the following:

> Is there anything more fundamental to human psychology than comfort seeking? Most of what we celebrate as societal progress involves the removal of discomfort-causing problems. Individually, we avoid situations in which we feel stressed—and with good reason: Stress is a killer. But in the modern world many of us have the luxury of insulating ourselves so thoroughly from stressors that we put ourselves at risk of adverse effects in the other direction. Untroubled by challenging experiences or information, we stop growing and learning. Our questioning capacity atrophies.[5]

As Gregersen discusses in his book *Questions Are the Answer*, most of us don't take the time to pause and ask ourselves (and others) what he refers to as "catalytic questions." We react instead of reflect. These questions act like catalysts in a chemical reaction, removing barriers to critical thinking and channeling energy to more productive pathways. Instead of taking the time to reflect and question, we often mistakenly believe we already have the answers—that is, the answer that offers the most comfortable, but not always best, solution.

This means getting comfortable with not having all the answers or letting go of previously held beliefs. Gregersen makes the point that creative questioners take time, often silently and in solitude, to clear their minds, reflect, and listen to their own thoughts. They then ask themselves the right questions.

This concept of silent thinking, questioning, and reflecting seems foreign in most businesses, as well as for most of us in our private lives. Gregersen cites the example of a leader in a European-based retail company who had been "caught thinking." As she leaned back in her office chair, the CEO walked by. He poked his head into the room and asked, "What are you doing?"

"Thinking," she replied.

"And when will you start *working*?"[6]

We aren't accustomed to the sound of silence. But intentionally giving ourselves the opportunity to reflect, ponder, and ask ourselves questions again and again gives us space to explore solutions. Granted, it's uncomfortable. But accept it. Make room for it. It's part of growth and exploration. The more you do it, the better you'll get.

HOW NOT TO SWIPE

Give yourself a break. Seriously. Give yourself a day off from the hot pursuit of your whatever-it-is lifelong dream, and don't wait until you're such a burnout case that you hate the thought of jumping back into that torment again. Plan your breaks, and don't feel guilty about them, for goodness' sake.

Pursuing a goal should not feel like a prison sentence; you're not chained to your desk until you complete your short-story collection, or to the weight bench until you complete one more set of bench presses. Taking a planned break from stressful, difficult work is not only therapeutic for mind and body but it's important to maintain high-quality performance too. When you step back from your goal for a day, you not only give your mind and body a chance to recover but you gain perspective on what you've already accomplished. It's also wise to use breaks as rewards for hard work or a job well done. There's a reason people in intensive weight-loss programs allow themselves "cheat days": your body and mind need the occasional reward to make self-deprivation possible the rest of the week and to avoid binging on bad behavior. So plan breaks for your physical and mental health, take them, and do not feel guilty about them.

5. Complete Something

Henry David Thoreau wrote: "We've wholly forgotten how to die. But be sure you do die, nevertheless. Do your work, and finish it. If you know how to begin, you will know when to end."[7] Seeing something through to completion, even if it's relatively small, can be a transformative event. That's especially true if you have a history of Swiping and not finishing what you start. Imagine the relief, the pride, in finally finishing something you've been failing to finish for years!

Quality is also beside the point. The new marathoner doesn't care if she finishes in seven hours, so long as she crosses the finish line. That's precisely the point of National Novel Writing Month. Most of those completed fifty-thousand-word manuscripts are not great, and some are downright terrible. But that doesn't matter, because quality is not the goal. Finishing something is. The rest will come.

As Harvard Business School professor Teresa Amabile and psychologist Steve Kramer point out in their book, *The Progress Principle*, a number of studies have found that it's not major life events that leave lasting effects on subjective well-being. Winning the lottery does not usually result in a lifetime of happiness. Rather, their studies found that it is the incremental successes and small advances that bring us joy. In fact, focusing solely on that "big, hairy, audacious goal," rather than on the small wins, often means we never finish what we start. Researchers Amabile and Kramer cite the following example: "People suffering from depression can find it difficult to maintain an exercise program, even though any kind of physical activity can reduce depressive symptoms. So, a goal like working out at the gym for an hour each day can seem unthinkable, and that workout never happens."[8]

The researchers also cite studies from Professor Daniel Mochon of the Sloan School of Management to illustrate their point. The studies found that individuals who accomplished a series of relatively minor activities over time, such as regularly attending religious services, regular exercise, or practicing yoga, felt happier after doing so, and those regular boosts from minor activities had a cumulative and lasting effect.

"Because setbacks are so common in truly important problems, people become disheartened unless they can point to some meaningful advance most days, even if that advance is seemingly minor, and even if it involves nothing more than extracting insights from the day's failures," state Amabile and Kramer. Small wins feel good, especially as they build up over the long run.

So get it on the cognitive whiteboard. Achieve even part of your goal. Savor it. It will help bring the MAGIC back. It will become addictive.

6. Repeat

Finally, after you have enjoyed the exultation of finishing something, knowing everything you had to overcome in order to get to this point, do it again. And again. And again. The beautiful thing about not Swiping—about the toolbox of skills, self-perceptions, mindfulness techniques, and cognitive tricks that you will develop by taking this alternate route around the Hamster Wheel—is that the more you use them—like a high-quality kitchen knife—the sharper and more effective they will become. If the Swipe has become your habit, create a new habit of completion.

We're not necessarily saying you need to jump right back into another challenging goal right away. After all, relishing your accomplishments, taking time off to recover, and enjoying the praise of others are some of the greatest pleasures of not Swiping. But use your newfound powers to take on something, even if it's small. Of course, if you're newly accomplished in a workplace setting, you may have no choice but to jump into another challenging, uncomfortable goal right away. That's one advantage and disadvantage of being in the professional world: You are regularly forced to confront your own perceived limitations and rise above them. If you're in that sort of workplace, accept the challenge and rise to the occasion. You will find your skills in completing things becoming even more well honed.

Or add on to the work you've just done. If you completed a short story, how about writing a novella next time? If you successfully trained for a 5K race, move to a 10K. Instead of attempting to resolve your communication problems with your teen by scheduling a one-month bonding retreat to the remote wilderness, start by going to dinner at her favorite restaurant. The trick is to get hooked on finishing things to the point where it's relatively effortless not to Swipe, and where you have a ready roster of strengths and processes that make getting to the finish line a smoother journey. As psychologist B. J. Fogg writes, start small, and anchor new habits in current practices. Enjoy the self-redefinition: You're no longer the person who's always talking about big goals but then failing to achieve them. You're the person who does what you set out to.

Arrest, Inquire, Evaluate, and Act

We know that Swiping is a habitual behavior ingrained in the brain's synaptic pathways by repeated activity, so how can you get past the aspirational stage and actually *stop Swiping*? How can you master your attention instead of mastering the Swipe? A three-part cognitive process may be the answer:

1. Arrest
2. Inquire
3. Evaluate and Act

Arrest

In order to have any hope of success in getting past the Swipe, you must halt that "reach for the eject button" impulse provoked by fear, discomfort, or panic. Accomplishing this requires you to do what in psychology is known as "creating space"—literally extending the time between the stimulus and your response to that stimulus. Gregersen's concept of asking questions can prove helpful here.

For instance, you might find yourself easily triggered by a workplace colleague's sloppy grammar in an important presentation, to the point where as soon as you see a typo you lash out with a withering remark. But because you're motivated by the desire to improve team cohesion—and the desire not to lose your job—you train yourself to take a few beats between the mistake and your response to it. You recognize your emotions flaring, and instead of snapping off a caustic remark you ask yourself why you're reacting this way. Having stopped your emotional reaction cold, you then offer useful feedback.

The alternative, where you don't instantly reach for your keyboard or phone like an Old West gunslinger reaching for his Colt .45 when someone says, "Draw," takes time and practice. But because it allows time for System Two of the brain to take the baton from the reflexive System One, such responses are more rational, more thoughtful, and usually more productive.

This is *arresting* the Swipe. When you recognize and stop the reactionary emotions behind Swiping, you gain the ability to be detached from what you're experiencing so you can notice your feelings in a nonjudgmental way. It's a state of mind akin to that of mindfulness meditation, in which the meditator is able to observe thoughts objectively rather than getting caught up in the stories behind them or passing judgment on them.

There are four parts to arresting the Swipe reflex:

1. **Plan ahead.** You will not always be able to arrest the impulse that leads to Swiping. Instead, anticipate the process that will occur when discomfort becomes overwhelming. Make the decision about what you will do before you get into that

situation. Then the decision will have already been made, and you won't have to remake it each time you face the challenge. You may feel shame, fear, self-disgust, or resignation, so anticipate it and recognize it when it arrives. That's how you'll be able to control your own narrative. When you can say, "Ah, I feel a Swipe coming on; this is what always happens," you're prepared for the feelings that descend on you and more able to deal with them.

2. **Recognize and confront your emotions.** Emotions are like cats: seeing them is one thing, but controlling them is a fight. In the beginning, as you're learning not to Swipe, you will almost certainly let your emotions get the best of you. Not to worry; defense against the Swipe is not rigid but elastic. More than once, you will find yourself being overtaken by grief, anger, or fear. But you can reach back and pull those emotions back into line. We know this is possible because of one group of people, billions strong, who confront their emotions and change their behavior on a regular basis: *parents*. When you have children, you have to change decades-long habits. No longer can you blithely curse around your toddler or let an explosive fit of temper terrify your kindergartener. Slowly, you begin to catch your volatile emotions in the act, slow down your reactions, and over time change your behavior. That reality leads us to one of the most important observations about the Swipe: *it is almost always reversible*. Even after you have Swiped away from law school, a serious relationship, or a challenging job, there's usually time to take it back. That's something many of us, wallowing in shame and remorse after Swiping for the umpteenth time, don't even consider. In the short term, a

Swipe is rarely permanent. As we stated in the beginning of the book, it can be fixed.

3. **Look at past lessons.** When you've Swiped in the past, what has it cost you? Did you feel foolish or ashamed? Did you lose a promotion? Did friends or coworkers give you a hard time? Did you lose a significant other or a career opportunity? Or did you bail out of a relationship at the first sign of disagreement? Most important, if you give into your emotions and Swipe now, will you suffer the same consequences again? Confronting past results of Swiping and extrapolating those results to the present can provide a powerful incentive *not* to Swipe—or, at least, to make a rational decision and tap out of a situation for the right reasons.

4. **Play it through to the end.** Psychologists use this concept to assist individuals confronting fears. But this technique, formally called "play the script till the end," is also a useful method to help us fight the Swipe reflex. Consider the consequences if the next action you take "plays through to the end," as if this were a movie. If you were to fast-forward after taking this particular action, what would be the most likely outcome? Would it be the outcome you want?

Let the physical sensations dissipate. In part, we experience emotions physically: the heat in the face of anger or embarrassment, the tingling in the stomach from anxiety, the pounding heart of fear. After you've identified and confronted the emotions that correlate with your Swipe, do nothing while they fade. When your heart stops pounding, your brain will stop creating the narrative that there's something to fear, and you will be less likely to fall victim to your fight-flight-freeze instinct. Instead, you'll be able to rationally analyze the situation and choose whether to walk away or stick with it. Allow System Two to kick in.

Inquire

Pausing the emotional chain reaction of the Swipe gives you space. Use that space to inquire about your motivations, feelings, and what's likely to happen if you—again—quit this pursuit that just a few weeks ago was the most important thing in your life.

Self-inquiry is the linchpin of a type of evidence-based talk therapy called Radically Open Dialectical Behavior Therapy (RO-DBT). Ideal for people who are highly self-controlling or inhibited, this is a kind of mindfulness practice in which you ask yourself questions to help you find your "edge"—the place where you have something to learn. The idea is to learn to understand yourself and your experiences from a new perspective and discover your blind spots.[9] For someone who's ridden the Hamster Wheel over and over again for years, this kind of questioning is ideal.

What kinds of questions? We're glad you asked:

- What do I want?
- Why did I want to do this in the first place?
- What progress have I made?
- What happens if I quit now?
- What happens if I keep going?
- What will be the likely result if I play this action through to the end?
- What's at stake? What will it cost me to quit?
- Am I doing this for myself, or to impress or prove something to certain people? How important are these people to me?

The possible questions you might ask yourself are limitless; these are merely suggestions. But all questions are a search for *evidence*. You're fishing around for data that will empower you to make a decision as opposed to Swiping. You're trying to put System Two completely in charge of what you do next.

HOW NOT TO SWIPE

- **Use desensitization training.** Astronauts train on the tasks and experiences of space flight until the very act of flying into orbit becomes so familiar it's almost mundane. The more you move past opportunities to Swipe, the more familiar you will become with the sensations involved, until you can predict them with perfect fidelity ("Here comes the Uphill, right on time!"). That will help them feel less dramatic and more like checkpoints.

- **The memory of persistence.** We couldn't resist the wordplay on the title of the famous Dali painting, but the advice is apt. Stop forcing yourself to do things you don't want to do out of the belief that persistence by itself is always a virtue. The "tap-out" proves that untrue. If you're truly not moved to continue something after multiple attempts, maybe it's just not for you.

- **Set prime stakes.** Sorry, the pun just called to us. Swiping can become so familiar that you get used to it, but if disengagement stops hurting—if it's become habit, character, and a part of who you are—then you're not setting the stakes for quitting high enough. Relationship therapists have a saying about leaving a dysfunctional relationship versus staying in it: "When the pain of staying is worse than the pain of leaving, you'll leave." Flip that on its head if you want to curb Swiping. Make the cost of quitting severe, and you're more likely to stick with it.

- **Finish something.** Doesn't matter how small it is, so long as it's productive and related to what you want to accomplish. Change your pattern and see something through to the end. One great example is the "Couch to 5K," a plan promoted by runners' groups and universities that promises to take someone from totally inactive to running a 5K race in just six weeks. Try something small but in the desired direction just to prove to yourself that yes, you can see something through to the end. It's not hopeless.

- **Change your environment and routine.** So you've tried six times to write a screenplay, each time working from your home office, and failed. Duh—get out of your home office! Do something to change things up: hire a personal trainer instead of working out on your own, write at Starbucks, get back into the office, etc.

- **Help someone else avoid Swiping.** If you're not ready to take the plunge, see what you've learned with a friend and help that person avoid Swiping and complete a cherished goal. You'll see that if this person can do it, so can you.

Evaluate and Act

In 2014 Satya Nadella became only the third CEO in Microsoft history, following two legends: Bill Gates and Steve Ballmer. He's quickly established his own legend credentials, however, by taking a company seen as stodgy and slow-moving in bold new directions, including domination of cloud computing in the form of the company's Azure platform. Part of Nadella's mandate came from his perception that Microsoft needed to go back to its core mission: building technology so that others can build technology.

He's also said that the giant corporation got a little full of itself, and it was this realization that led him to reorient the Microsoft culture. "In '98 we became the world's largest-market-cap company," Nadella said in a Stanford interview. "You could see people walking around like, 'Wow, we must be God's gift to mankind.' [Instead] I wanted a culture that reflected a learning organization."[10]

Evaluating the answers to questions and acting on the relevant data is part of *evidence-based management*. Businesses prone to Swipe away from difficult challenges, or that have MAGIC-deficient cultures that discourage their people to pursue failure and embrace discomfort, would certainly benefit from this approach.

Evaluating the information gained from inquiry naturally leads to action, completing the swerve away from reflexive System One outcomes in favor of System Two agency and choice. When you've asked all the questions you find relevant to your situation and considered the possible answers, it's time to decide what those answers imply for the only thing that matters: *what you do next*. Based on what you learn from inquiry and contemplation of answers, should you continue toward your goal, or does it make more sense for you to tap out and return to the goal later or tap out altogether? Does the pursuit make sense at this time, and is it truly something you want? If you were to continue moving toward the finish line, would conditions need to change? Do your expectations need to change?

Evaluate everything you've learned, chart your course, and do whatever makes the most sense to you, even if that means tapping out. Remember: as long as you are moving toward something new, there's nothing wrong with walking away from what's not right.

What Happens When We Don't Swipe?

When we consider the millions of personal and professional goals unreached because of the Swipe, it is not a stretch to say that widespread ending of the Swipe could potentially change society on a personal and a business level.

Imagine what is possible. An end to the futility and frustration of consistently starting and then stopping in the pursuit of important goals and milestones. Finally slaying personal demons and overcoming challenges once thought to be impossible. A collection of accomplishments at every level of society, from people completing college educations and reaching health and fitness goals to artists and entrepreneurs creating new and amazing things. Given the power of shame and resentment, millions more people bypassing the Swipe to reengage in their most valued goals might transform morale and self-esteem in our society.

In a business context, the transformation might be even more profound. Imagine teams and departments and thousands of organizations across the country, from corporations and hospitals to universities and churches, that function with greater self-awareness, leading to higher productivity. Imagine corporate cultures in which everyone is encouraged to pursue brave failures and lean into discomfort. Instead of a rash of resignations, challenge and difficulty in the workplace can lead to greater employee retention as organizational cultures change to encourage people to confront their fears in order to rise above them. Employee engagement might well soar, and individual growth and professional development would likely do the same as individuals from the newest hires all the way to the C-suite would find the support and tools they need to increase their self-awareness, confront discomfort and difficulty, and discover new capacities.

If Swiping locks up untapped potential behind steel bars and concrete walls, imagine the epic flood of potential that would be unleashed if just a fraction of us stopped Swiping and finished what we started. Imagine the transformation of health care if more of us took better care of ourselves and attained greater fitness. Imagine the economic growth if more apprehensive entrepreneurs went for it and started the companies they've been doodling on napkins. Imagine the innovation, the conversation, the vast improvements in mental health when millions feel courageous and empowered at the end of the day rather than humiliated and diminished. Imagine the possibilities and self-fulfillment if we reengaged in our jobs, our families, our social connections, our bucket lists, our hobbies— our lives.

Imagine what we could do. Imagine what *you* could do. Now stop imagining.

Endnotes

Introduction

1   Harris, Margaret, and George Butterworth. *Developmental Psychology*. Psychology Press, 2012, 114.

2   Sommerville, J. A., Woodward, A. L., and Needham, A. (2005). "Action experience alters 3-month-old infants' perception of others' actions." *Cognition*, 96(1), B1–B11. https://doi.org/10.1016/j.cognition.2004.07.004.

3   Material Design, https://material.io/design/interaction/gestures.html#properties, retrieved May 10, 2020.

4   Pallardy, Richard. "The Psychology of Swiping in Apps," App Partner, August 21, 2018, https://www.apppartner.com/the-psychology-of-swiping-in-apps/.

5   Maylett, T. (2019). *Engagement MAGIC: Five Keys for Engaging People, Leaders, and Organizations*. Austin: Greenleaf Book Group.

6   DNA of Engagement. The Conference Board. (n.d.). Retrieved June 10, 2022, from https://www.conference-board.org/topics/dna-of-engagement.

Chapter 1

1   Ferrari, J. R., Johnson, J. L., and McCown, W. G. (1995). *Procrastination and Task Avoidance*. Springer Publishing.

2   Schwantes, Marcel. "Science Says 92 Percent of People Don't Achieve Their Goals. Here's How the Other 8 Percent Do," *Inc.* https://www.inc.com/mar-cel-schwantes/science-says-92-percent-of-people-dont-achieve-goals-heres-how-the-other-8-perce.html, retrieved June 20, 2021.

3   Choi, Catherine. "New Year's resolution statistics," Finder, December 4, 2020, https://www.finder.com/new-years-resolution-statistics, retrieved June 20, 2021.

4   Iacurci, G. (2022, March 22). "The great resignation continues, as 44% of workers look for a new job." CNBC. Retrieved June 11, 2022, from https://www.cnbc.com/2022/03/22/great-resignation-continues-as-44percent-of-workers-seek-a-new-job.html.

5   Moesgaard, Simon. "The Zeigarnik Effect: The Tendency to Complete Things That Were Left Incomplete," Reflectd, August 14, 2013, https://reflectd.co/2013/08/14/the-zeigarnik-effect-the-tendency-to-complete-things-that-were-left-incomplete/, retrieved June 23, 2021.

6   Savitsky, Kenneth, Victoria Husted Medvec, and Thomas Gilovich. "Remembering and Regretting: The Zeigarnik Effect and the Cognitive Availability of Regrettable Actions and Inactions." *Personality and Social Psychology Bulletin* 23, no. 3 (March 1997): 248–57. https://doi.org/10.1177/0146167297233004.

7   Ellis, S. G. (n.d.). "Do we trust him? Hard is good." The Church of Jesus Christ of Latter-day Saints. Retrieved July 13, 2022, from https://www.churchofjesuschrist.org/study/general-conference/2017/10/do-we-trust-him-hard-is-good?lang=eng.

Chapter 2

1   Yin, Y., Wang, Y., Evans, J. A., and Wang, D. (2019). "Quantifying the dynamics of failure across science, startups and security." *Nature*, 575(7781), 190–194. https://doi.org/10.1038/s41586-019-1725-y.

2   Taylor, Alan. "Winners of the 2014 National Geographic Photo Contest," *Atlantic*, December 18, 2014, https://www.theatlantic.com/photo/2014/12/winners-of-the-2014-national-geographic-photo-contest/100875/#img01, retrieved September 28, 2021.

3   Dalla-Camina, Megan. "The Reality of Imposter Syndrome," *Psychology Today*, September 3, 2018, https://www.psychologytoday.com/us/blog/real-women/201809/the-reality-imposter-syndrome, retrieved September 17, 2021.

4   Volpp, K. G., John, L. K., Troxel, A. B., Norton, L., Fassbender, J., Loewenstein, G. "Financial Incentive–Based Approaches for Weight Loss: A Randomized Trial." *JAMA*. 2008; 300(22):2631–2637. doi:10.1001/jama.2008.804.

5   Frederickson, J. (2017). *The Lies We Tell Ourselves: How to Face the Truth, Accept Yourself, and Create a Better Life.* Seven Leaves Press.

Chapter 3

1   Murphy, S. C., and Bastian, B. (2019). "Emotionally extreme life experiences are more meaningful." *Journal of Positive Psychology*, 15(4), 531–542. https://doi.org/10.1080/17439760.2019.1639795.

2   Rozin, P., Guillot, L., Fincher, K., Rozin, A., and Tsukayama, E. (2013). "Glad to be sad, and other examples of benign masochism." *Judgment and Decision Making*, 8(4), 439–447.

3   Steber, Carolyn. "15 Things Psychologists Wish You Knew Can Gradually Destroy Self-Esteem," *Bustle*, December 20, 2017, https://www.bustle.com/p/15-things-psychologists-wish-you-knew-can-gradually-destroy-self-esteem-7611332, retrieved October 12, 2021.

4   "Attempts to Lose Weight Among Adults in the United States, 2013–2016," Centers for Disease Control and Prevention, https://www.cdc.gov/nchs/products/databriefs/db313.htm.

5   Brown, B. (2021). *Daring Greatly: How the Courage to Be Vulnerable Transforms the Way We Live, Love, Parent, and Lead.* Portfolio.

6   Tougas F., Lagacé M., Laplante J., Bellehumeur C. "Shielding self-esteem through the adoption of psychological disengagement mechanisms: the good and the bad news." *International Journal of Aging and Human Development*. 2008;67(2):129–48. doi: 10.2190/AG.67.2.b. PMID: 20063847.

7   Devaney, Tim. "Nearly 40% of millennials overspend to keep up with friends," Credit Karma, April 5, 2018, https://www.creditkarma.com/insights/i/fomo-spending-affects-one-in-four-millennials, retrieved October 11, 2021.

8   Gordon, Sherri. "How FOMO Impacts Teens and Young Adults," *Verywell Family*, November 30, 2020, https://www.verywellfamily.com/how-fomo-impacts-teens-and-young-adults-4174625, retrieved October 13, 2021.

9   Morin, Amy. "10 Reasons Teens Have So Much Anxiety Today," *Psychology Today*, November 3, 2017, https://www.psychologytoday.com/us/blog/what-mentally-strong-people-dont-do/201711/10-reasons-teens-have-so-much-anxiety-today?eml, retrieved October 5, 2021.

10   Coyne, S. M., Shawcroft, J., Gale, M., Gentile, D. A., Etherington, J. T., Holmgren, H., and Stockdale, L. (2021). "Tantrums, toddlers and technology: Temperament, media emotion regulation, and problematic media use in early childhood." *Computers in Human Behavior*, *120*, 106762. https://doi.org/10.1016/j.chb.2021.106762.

11   Harvard Youth Poll, 41st Edition, Spring 2021, Harvard Kennedy School, https://iop.harvard.edu/youth-poll/spring-2021-harvard-youth-poll.

12   Deering, Shelby. "How to Escape an 'I Give Up' Mindset," Talkspace, October 8, 2020, https://www.talkspace.com/blog/i-give-up-depression-anxiety/, retrieved October 20, 2021.

13   The Mental Health Million Project, Sapien Labs, https://sapienlabs.org/mental-health-million-project.

14   Hall, Judith; Leary, Mark. "The U.S. Has an Empathy Deficit," *Scientific American*, September 17, 2020, https://www.scientificamerican.com/article/the-us-has-an-empathy-deficit/, retrieved October 14, 2021.

15   Tettegah, S. Y., and Espelage, D. L. (2015). *Emotions, Technology, and Behaviors (Emotions and Technology)* (1st ed.). Academic Press.

Chapter 4

1   Henley, J. (2016, February 12). "Long lunch: Spanish civil servant skips work for years without anyone noticing." Retrieved from https://www.theguardian.com/world/2016/feb/12/long-lunch-spanish-civil-servant-skips-work-for-years-without-anyone-noticing.

2   "Over 50% of US Workers Are Thinking About a New Job for the New Year," Indeed.com, January 14, 2016. Retrieved from http://blog.indeed.com/2016/01/14/new-jobfor-the-new-year/.

3   Cook, I. (2021, November 10). "Who is driving the great resignation?" *Harvard Business Review*. Retrieved March 3, 2022, from https://hbr.org/2021/09/who-is-driving-the-great-resignation.

4   Simkin, J. (n.d.). "The Roman Army." Spartacus Educational. Retrieved March 3, 2022, from https://spartacus-educational.com/ROMarmy.htm.

5   Polybius, Scott-Kilvert, I., and Walbank, F. W. (2003). *The Rise of the Roman Empire*. Penguin.

6   Maylett, T., and Wride, M. (2017). *The Employee Experience: How to Attract Talent, Retain Top Performers, and Drive Results*. Hoboken, New Jersey: Wiley.

7   Smith, William (2006-07-14). Smith (1901) *Dictionary of Greek and Roman Antiquities, Vol. 1*, 797.

8   Maylett, T. (2019). *Engagement MAGIC: Five Keys for Engaging People, Leaders, and Organizations*. Austin: Greenleaf Book Group, 52.

9   DecisionWise. (2019, July 9). "5 personal benefits of employee engagement." DecisionWise. Retrieved March 5, 2022, from https://decision-wise.com/5-personal-benefits-employee-engagement/.

10   Rath, T., and Harter, J. K. (2010). *Wellbeing: The Five Essential Elements*. Gallup Press.

11   Oswald, Andrew J., Proto, Eugenio, and Sgroi, Daniel. (2015) "Happiness and productivity." *Journal of Labor Economics*, 33(4). 789–822.

12   Sons, M., and Niessen, C. (2021). "Cross-lagged effects of voluntary job changes and well-being: A continuous time approach." *Journal of Applied Psychology*. https://doi.org/10.1037/apl0000940.

13   Matuson, R. (2021, December 6). "So you want to quit your brand-new job," *Harvard Business Review*. Retrieved March 5, 2022, from https://hbr.org/2021/12/so-you-want-to-quit-your-brand-new-job.

14   Goler, L., Gale, J., Harrington, B., and Grant, A. (2018, January 11). "Why people really quit their jobs." *Harvard Business Review*. Retrieved March 5, 2022, from https://hbr.org/2018/01/why-people-really-quit-their-jobs.

15   Grant, Adam. "Title of the Podcast Episode." *Worklife with Adam Grant*, TED, Spotify, https://t.co/RFaG2X31i4, retrieved March 4, 2022 from https://twitter.com/adammgrant/status/1376875220569579520?.

16   US CIA. (1944, January 17). *Simple Sabotage Field Manual*. Homeland Security Digital Library, https://www.cia.gov/,. Retrieved March 5, 2022, from https://www.hsdl.org/?abstract&did=750070.

17   Maylett, T. (2019). *Engagement MAGIC: Five Keys for Engaging People, Leaders, and Organizations*. Austin: Greenleaf Book Group, 24.

18   Lebow, H. (2021, November 5). "Are you sabotaging yourself? Here's how to know and what to do." Psych Central. Retrieved March 5, 2022, from https://psychcentral.com/blog/overcome-self-sabotage.

19   Achor, S., Reece, A., Kellerman, G., and Robichaux, A. (2018, November 6). "9 Out of 10 People Are Willing to Earn Less Money to Do More-Meaningful Work." *Harvard Business Review*. Retrieved March 2, 2022, from https://hbr.org/2018/11/9-out-of-10-people-are-willing-to-earn-less-money-to-do-more-meaningful-work.

20   Hess, A. (2019, February 27). "LinkedIn: 94% of employees say they would stay at a company longer for this reason-and it's not a raise." CNBC. Retrieved March 1, 2022, from https://www.cnbc.com/2019/02/27/94percent-of-employees-would-stay-at-a-company-for-this-one-reason.html.

21 Maylett, T. (2019). *Engagement MAGIC: Five Keys for Engaging People, Leaders, and Organizations*. Austin: Greenleaf Book Group, 128.

22 Glassdoor, Harris Interactive (2019). "The Age of Social Recruiting."

23 Nicholas A. Christakis and James H. Fowler. "The Spread of Obesity in a Large Social Network over 32 Years," *New England Journal of Medicine* 357, (July 26, 2007): 370–79.

Chapter 5

1 Pychyl, T. A.; Lee, J. M.; Thibodeau, R.; Blunt, A. *Journal of Social Behavior and Personality*; Corte Madera, CA Vol. 15, Iss. 5, (Jan 1, 2000): 239.

2 Kader, Ruhul. "Why We Don't Finish What We Start—a Psychological Exploration," Future Startup, November 2, 2020, https://futurestartup. com/2020/11/02/why-we-dont-finish-what-we-start, retrieved September 2, 2021.

3 Locke, Edwin A., and Gary P. Latham. "New Directions in Goal-Setting Theory." *Current Directions in Psychological Science* 15, no. 5 (October 2006): 265–68. https://doi.org/10.1111/j.1467-8721.2006.00449.x.

4 Gardner, Sarah and Albee, Dave, "Study focuses on strategies for achieving goals, resolutions" (2015). Press Releases. 266.

5 Lunenburg, Fred. "Goal-Setting Theory of Motivation," *International Journal Of Management, Business, and Administration*, volume 15, Number 1, 2011.

6 Sharot, T. (2011). "The optimism bias." *Current Biology, 21*(23), R941–R945. https://doi.org/10.1016/j.cub.2011.10.030.

7 Morris, Errol (20 June 2010). "The Anosognosic's Dilemma: Something's Wrong but You'll Never Know What It Is (Part 1)." *New York Times*. Retrieved 7 March2011.

8 Tomalin, N., and Hall, R. (2017). *The Strange Last Voyage of Donald Crowhurst* (Illustrated ed.). Quercus.

9 Bryson, Bill. *A Walk in the Woods: Rediscovering America on the Appalachian Trail*. (1999). Broadway; 1st edition.

10 Barton, William. "Down in the Dark," *Asimov's Science Fiction*, December 1998.

Chapter 6

1   Adrian F. Ward, Kristen Duke, Ayelet Gneezy, and Maarten W. Bos. "Brain Drain: The Mere Presence of One's Own Smartphone Reduces Available Cognitive Capacity," *Journal of the Association for Consumer Research*, 2017, 2:2, 140–154.

2   Clary Davies, John. "Screen Savior," *Outside*, September 2021, 30.

3   Wang, Y. (2013, March 25). "More people have cell phones than toilets, U.N. study shows." *Time*. Retrieved June 10, 2022, from https://newsfeed.time.com/2013/03/25/more-people-have-cell-phones-than-toilets-u-n-study-shows/.

4   Daniel Miller, Laila Abed Rabho, Patrick Awondo, Maya de Vries, Marília Duque, Pauline Garvey, Laura Haapio-Kirk, Charlotte Hawkins, Alfonso Otaegui, Shireen Walton, and Xinyuan Wang. *The Global Smartphone: Beyond a Youth Technology*, London: UCL Press, May 2021.

5   Hern, Alex. "Smartphone is now 'the place where we live', anthropologists say," *Guardian*, May 10, 2021, https://www.theguardian.com/technology/2021/may/10/smartphone-is-now-the-place-where-we-live-anthropologists-say, retrieved October 3, 2021.

6   Willis, Janine, and Alexander Todorov. "First Impressions: Making Up Your Mind After a 100-Ms Exposure to a Face." *Psychological Science* 17, no. 7 (July 2006): 592–98. https://doi.org/10.1111/j.1467-9280.2006.01750.x.

7   Carr, Nicholas. "How Smartphones Hijack Our Minds," *Wall Street Journal*, October 6, 2017, https://www.wsj.com/articles/how-smartphones-hijack-our-minds-1507307811, retrieved October 10, 2021.

Chapter 7

1   Baumeister, R. F., Vohs, K. D., Aaker, J. L., and Garbinsky, E. N. (2013). "Some key differences between a happy life and a meaningful life." *Journal of Positive Psychology*, 8(6), 505–516. https://doi.org/10.1080/17439760.2013.830764.

2   Murphy, Sean, Bastian, Brock. 2019/07/17; 1, 12 "Emotionally extreme life experiences are more meaningful." *Journal of Positive Psychology*. https://www.researchgate.net/publication/334526863_Emotionally_extreme_life_experiences_are_more_meaningful/citation/download.

3   https://www.amazon.com/Religions-Values-Peak-Experiences-Abraham-Maslow/dp/8087888847.

4   https://blogs.scientificamerican.com/beautiful-minds/emotional-ly-extreme-experiences-not-just-positive-or-negative-experienc-es-are-more-meaningful-in-life.

5   https://static1.squarespace.com/static/5db8a4995630c6238cbb4c26/t/5ecc11 4b250a6a0b1ab056e7/1590432078145/Valoir+Report+-+The+real+produc-tivity+impact+of+remote+work.pdf.

6   https://news.harvard.edu/gazette/story/2010/11/wandering-mind-not-a-happy-mind/.

7   https://www.nytimes.com/2020/09/26/at-home/how-to-get-focused.htm-l?smid=em-share.

8   *Thinking, Fast and Slow*, Daniel Kahneman, published by Farrar, Straus and Giroux, LLC. 2011.

9   Bandura, A (1977). "Self-efficacy: Toward a Unifying Theory of Behavioral Change." *Psychological Review*. 84(2): 191–215.

10 Bandura, Albert (1982). "Self-efficacy mechanism in human agency." *American Psychologist*. 37(2): 122–147.

11 Aldao, A. et al. "Emotion-Regulation Strategies Across Psychopathology: A Meta-Analytic Review." *Clinical Psychology Review* 30, no. 2, 217–37 (2010). https://doi.org/10.1016/j.cpr.2009.11.004.

12 Weisberg, Deena Skolnick; et al. (June 2014). *"Mise en place: setting the stage for thought and action"* (PDF). Trends in Cognitive Sciences. 18 (6): 276-278. doi:10.1016/j.tics.2014.02.012. PMID 24684854. S2CID 35633523.

13 Sarah M. Coyne, Adam A. Rogers, Jessica D. Zurcher, Laura Stockdale, McCall Booth. "Does time spent using social media impact mental health?: An eight-year longitudinal study," *Computers in Human Behavior*, Volume 104, 2020, 106–160, https://doi.org/10.1016/j.chb.2019.106160.

14 Ward, A. F., Duke, K., Gneezy, A. and Bos, M. W. (2017). "Brain Drain: The Mere Presence of One's Own Smartphone Reduces Available Cognitive Capacity." *Journal of the Association for Consumer Research*, Vol. 2(2), https://doi.org/10.1086/691462.

15 Burak, Lydia (2012). "Multitasking in the University Classroom." *International Journal for the Scholarship of Teaching and Learning*: Vol. 6: No. 2, (8).

16 Pink, D. H. (2022). *The Power of Regret: How Looking Backward Moves Us Forward* (23–24), Riverhead Books.

17 Shimanoff, Susan B. "Commonly named emotions in everyday conversations." Perceptual and Motor Skills (1984).

18 https://www.psychologytoday.com/us/blog/the-mindful-self-express/201205/the-psychology-regret.

19 https://theconversation.com/regret-can-be-all-consuming-a-neurobehav-ioral-scientist-explains-how-people-can-overcome-it-172466.

20 Ibid.

Chapter 8

1 lwilliams@mlive.com, L. W. (2021, March 20). *NBA official Jenna Schroeder looks to spread the word that refereeing could be a career.* mlive. Retrieved February 3, 2022, from https://www.mlive.com/pistons/2021/03/nba-offi-cial-jenna-schroeder-looks-to-spread-the-word-that-refereeing-could-be-a-career.html.

2 *SportsCenter.* (2019, November 24). "This ref has wheels." Twitter. Retrieved February 3, 2022, from https://twitter.com/SportsCenter/status/1198722597464264707.

3 Ross, V. (2019, October 17). "Numbers: The nervous system, from 268-MPH signals to trillions of synapses." *Discover.* Retrieved February 3, 2022, from https://www.discovermagazine.com/health/numbers-the-nervous-system-from-268-mph-signals-to-trillions-of-synapses.

4 Xu et al., 2017, *Neuron* 96, 1447–1458 December 20, 2017, Elsevier. https://doi.org/10.1016/j.neuron.2017.11.010.

5 Williams R. W., Herrup K. "The control of neuron number." *Annual Review of Neuroscience.* 1988; 11:423–53. doi 10.1146/annurev.ne.11.030188.002231. PMID: 3284447.

6 Herculano-Houzel, S. "The human brain in numbers: a linearly scaled-up primate brain." *Frontiers in Human Neuroscience.* 2009; 3:31. doi:10.3389/neuro.09.031.2009.

7 R. Marois and J. Ivanoff. "Capacity Limits of Information Processing in the Brain," *Trends in Cognitive Sciences* 9, no. 6 (2005): 296–305.

8 Ross, V. (2019, October 17). "Numbers: The nervous system, from 268-MPH signals to trillions of synapses." *Discover.* Retrieved February 3, 2022, from https://www.discovermagazine.com/health/numbers-the-nervous-system-from-268-mph-signals-to-trillions-of-synapses.

9 "Petabyte - how much information could it actually hold?"(n.d.). Retrieved February 3, 2022, from https://info.cobaltiron.com/blog/peta-byte-how-much-information-could-it-actually-hold.

10 Ackerman, S. *Discovering the Brain*, Washington, DC: National Academies Press (US); 1992.

11 Gazzaley, A., and Rosen, L. D. (2016). *The Distracted Mind: Ancient brains in a High-Tech World*. MIT Press, 19.

12 Herculano-Houzel, S. "Do you know your brain? A survey on public neuroscience literacy at the closing of the decade of the brain." *Neuroscientist*. 2002 Apr;8(2):98–110. doi: 10.1177/107385840200800206. PMID: 11954564.

13 Herculano-Houzel, S. (2009). "The human brain in numbers: a linearly scaled-up primate brain." *Frontiers in Human Neuroscience* 3(31). https://doi.org/10.3389/neuro.09.031.2009.

14 https://www.forbes.com/sites/bendowsett/2019/05/01/the-nbas-referee-problem-will-last-as-long-as-we-want-it-to/?sh=5839f2a974b7.

15 Jha, A. (2021). *Peak Mind: Find Your Focus, Own Your Attention, Invest 12 Minutes a Day*. HarperOne, an imprint of HarperCollins, Publishers, 28.

16 Jha, A. (2021). *Peak Mind: Find Your Focus, Own Your Attention, Invest 12 Minutes a Day*. HarperOne, an imprint of HarperCollins, Publishers, 33.

17 Killingsworth, M. A., and Gilbert, D. T. "A Wandering Mind Is an Unhappy Mind." *Science* 330, no. 6006, 932 (2010).

18 Kane, M. J., et al. "For Whom the Mind Wanders, and When: An Experience-Sampling Study of Working Memory and Executive Control in Daily Life." *Psychological Science* 18, no. 7, 614–21 (2007). https://doi.org/10.1111/j.1467–9280.2007.01948.x.

19 Broadway, J. M. et al. "Early Event-Related Brain Potentials and Hemispheric Asymmetries Reveal Mind-Wandering While Reading and Predict Comprehension." *Biological Psychology* 107, 31–43 (2015). http://dx.doi.org/10.1016/j.biopsycho.2015.02.009.

20 Hogan, Lilianna. "How Daydreaming Can Be Good For You," WebMD, September 14, 2021, https://www.webmd.com/balance/features/why-does-daydreaming-get-such-bad-rap, retrieved February 14, 2022.

21 Jha, A. (2021). *Peak Mind: Find Your Focus, Own Your Attention, Invest 12 Minutes a Day*. HarperOne, an imprint of HarperCollins, Publishers, 93–94.

22 Smallwood, J., et al. "The Lights Are On but No One's Home: Meta-Awareness and the Decoupling of Attention When the Mind Wanders." *Psychonomic Bulletin & Review* 14, no. 3, 527–33 (2007). https://doi.org/10.3758/BF03194102.

23 Fox News, "Air Force strips 17 officers of power to launch intercontinental nuclear missiles," May 8, 2013, http://www.foxnews.com/politics/2013/05/08/air-force-reportedly-strips-17-officers-power-to-launch-intercontinental/.

24 Robert Burns. "Nuclear officers napped with blast door left open," Associated Press, October 23, 2013.

25 https://www.cnn.com/2008/US/08/29/airforce.sanctions/.

26 Esterman, M., et al. "In the Zone or Zoning Out? Tracking Behavioral and Neural Fluctuations During Sustained Attention." *Cerebral Cortex* 23, no. 11, 2712–23 (2013). https://doi.org/10.1093/cercor/bhs261. Mrazek, M. D. et al.

27 https://crashstats.nhtsa.dot.gov/Api/Public/ViewPublication/813060.

28 James, William. *Mind*, vol. 9, no. 33 (January 1884), 1–26.

29 E. Garcia-Rill. "Reticular Activating System," Editor(s): Larry R. Squire, Encyclopedia of Neuroscience, Academic Press, 2009, Pages 137–143, https://doi.org/10.1016/B978-008045046-9.01767-8.

30 Gazzaley, A., and Rosen, L. D. (2016). *The Distracted Mind: Ancient Brains in a High-Tech World*. MIT Press, 13.

31 T. T. Hills. "Animal Foraging and the Evolution of Goal-Directed Cognition," *Cognitive Science* 30, no. 1 (2006): 3–14.

32 Gazzaley, A., and Rosen, L. D. (2016). *The Distracted Mind: Ancient Brains in a High-Tech World*. MIT Press, 14.

33 Jha, A. (2021). *Peak Mind: Find Your Focus, Own Your Attention, Invest 12 Minutes a Day*. HarperOne, an imprint of HarperCollins, Publishers, 98.

34 Lavie, N. et al. "Load Theory of Selective Attention and Cognitive Control." *Journal of Experimental Psychology* 133, no. 3, 339–54 (2004). https://doi.org/10.1037/0096-3445.133.3.339.

35 Chabris, C., and Simons, D. (2010). *The Invisible Gorilla: Thinking Clearly in a World of Illusions*. Crown.

36 Magazine, S. (2012, September 1). "But did you see the gorilla? The problem with inattentional blindness." Smithsonian.com. Retrieved February 3, 2022, from https://www.smithsonianmag.com/science-nature/but-did-you-see-the-gorilla-the-problem-with-inattentional-blindness-17339778/.

37 Gazzaley, A., and Rosen, L. D. (2016). *The Distracted Mind: Ancient Brains in a High-Tech World*. MIT Press, 131.

38 Strayer, D. L., Watson, J. M., and Drews, F. A. (2011). "Cognitive distraction while multitasking in the automobile." *Advances in Research and Theory* 54, 29–58. https://doi.org/10.1016/b978-0-12-385527-5.00002-4.

39 Shapiro, F., 2021. *The New Yale Book of Quotations*. New Haven: Yale University Press, 716.

40 Posner, M. I., and Driver, J. "The Neurobiology of Selective Attention." *Current Opinion in Neurobiology* 2, no. 2, 165–69 (1992). https://doi.org/10.1016/0959-4388(92)90006-7.

41 Smallwood, J., et al. "Segmenting the Stream of Consciousness: The Psychological Correlates of Temporal Structures in the Time Series Data of a Continuous Performance Task." *Brain and Cognition* 66, no. 1, 50–56 (2008). https://doi.org/10.1016/j.bandc.2007.05.004.

42 Polychroni, N., et al. "Response Time Fluctuations in the Sustained Attention to Response Task Predict Performance Accuracy and Meta-Awareness of Attentional States." *Psychology of Consciousness: Theory, Research, and Practice* (2020). https://doi.org/10.1037/cns0000248.

Chapter 9

1   Gazzaley, A., and Rosen, L. D. (2016). *The Distracted Mind: Ancient Brains in a High-Tech World.* MIT Press, 79.

2   Nass, C. (2009, August 24). "Multitaskers bad at multitasking." BBC News. Retrieved February 4, 2022, from http://news.bbc.co.uk/2/hi/technology/8219212.stm.

3   McSpadden, K. (2015, May 14). "Science: You now have a shorter attention span than a goldfish." *Time.* Retrieved February 4, 2022, from https://time.com/3858309/attention-spans-goldfish/.

4   David, P., Kim, J. H., Brickman, J. S., Ran, W., and Curtis, C. M. (2014). "Mobile phone distraction while studying." *New Media & Society* 17(10), 1661–1679. https://doi.org/10.1177/1461444814531692.

5   Gazzaley, A., and Rosen, L. D. (2016). *The Distracted Mind: Ancient Brains in a High-Tech World.* MIT Press, 77.

6   Taylor, J. (2011, March 30). "Technology: Myth of multitasking." *Psychology Today.* Retrieved February 4, 2022, from https://www.psychologytoday.com/us/blog/the-power-prime/201103/technology-myth-multitasking.

7   Gazzaley, A., and Rosen, L. D. (2016). *The Distracted Mind: Ancient Brains in a High-Tech World.* MIT Press, 62.

8   Zee News. (2012, April 10). "Consumers in their 20s Switch Media 27 times an hour." Zee News. Retrieved March 11, 2022, from https://zeenews.india.com/business/news/technology/consumers-in-their-20s-switch-media-27-times-an-hour_50655.html.

9   Cowan N. (2014). "Working Memory Underpins Cognitive Development, Learning, and Education." *Educational Psychology Review* 26(2), 197–223. https://doi.org/10.1007/s10648-013-9246-y.

10   Jha, A. (2021). *Peak Mind: Find Your Focus, Own Your Attention, Invest 12 Minutes a Day*. HarperOne, an imprint of HarperCollins, Publishers.

11   "Brain games: inside the brain of the elite athlete." (2016, September 8). Queensland Brain Institute—University of Queensland. https://qbi.uq.edu.au/blog/2016/09/brain-games-inside-brain-elite-athlete/.

12   Zee News. (2012, April 10). "Consumers in their 20s Switch Media 27 times an hour." Zee News. Retrieved March 11, 2022, from https://zeenews.india.com/business/news/technology/consumers-in-their-20s-switch-media-27-times-an-hour_50655.html.

13   Maguire, E. A., Woollett, K., and Spiers, H. J. (2006). "London taxi drivers and bus drivers: A structural MRI and neuropsychological analysis." *Hippocampus* 16(12), 1091–1101. https://doi.org/10.1002/hipo.20233.

14   Kim W, Chang Y, Kim J, Seo J, Ryu K, Lee E, Woo M, Janelle CM. "An fMRI study of differences in brain activity among elite, expert, and novice archers at the moment of optimal aiming." *Cognitive and Behavioral Neurology*. 2014 Dec; 27(4):173–82. doi: 10.1097/WNN.0000000000000042. PMID: 25539036.

15   Macnamara, B. N., and Maitra, M. (2019). "The role of deliberate practice in expert performance: revisiting Ericsson, Krampe & Tesch-Römer" (1993). *Royal Society Open Science* 6(8), 190327. https://doi.org/10.1098/rsos.190327.

16   Gazzaley, A., and Rosen, L. D. (2016). *The Distracted Mind: Ancient Brains in a High-Tech World*. MIT Press, 183.

Chapter 10

1   Chen, Angela. "A psychologist explains why we're probably all delusional and how to fix it," *Verge*, May 21, 2017, https://www.theverge.com/2017/5/21/15660894/insight-self-awareness-psychology-tasha-eurich-interview, retrieved October 24, 2021.

2   Stephen R. Covey. *The Seven Habits of Highly Effective People: Restoring the Character Ethic* (New York: Simon & Schuster, 1989), 70.

3   Hall, Leanne. "Why Accepting Discomfort Improves Your Emotional Health," Open Colleges, March 15, 2016, https://www.opencolleges.edu.au/careers/blog/how-why-accepting-discomfort-improves-your-emotional-health, retrieved October 22, 2021.

4   Murakami, Haruki, and Philip Gabriel. 2005. *Kafka on the Shore*. London: Harvill.

5   Gregersen, H. B. (2018). *Questions Are the Answer: A Breakthrough Approach to Your Most Vexing Problems at Work and in Life* (127). HarperBusiness, an imprint of HarperCollins Publishers.

6   Gregersen, H. B. (2018). *Questions Are the Answer: A Breakthrough Approach to Your Most Vexing Problems at Work and in Life* (167). HarperBusiness, an imprint of HarperCollins Publishers.

7   Thoreau, Henry David. *A Yankee in Canada: With Anti-Slavery and Reform Papers* (ed. 1866).

8   Amabile, Teresa, and Steve Kramer. (2014, July 23). "Small wins and feeling good." *Harvard Business Review*. Retrieved June 13, 2022, from https://hbr.org/2011/05/small-wins-and-feeling-good.

9   "Self-control—the ability to inhibit competing urges, impulses, behaviors, or desires and delay gratification in order to pursue future goals," Radically Open, https://www.radicallyopen.net/about-ro-dbt/, retrieved October 22, 2021.

10   Waikar, Sachin. "Microsoft CEO Satya Nadella: Be Bold and Be Right," Stanford Graduate School of Business, November 26, 2019, https://www.gsb.stanford.edu/insights/microsoft-ceo-satya-nadella-be-bold-be-right, retrieved October 27, 2021.

About the Authors

Tracy Maylett, Ed.D, is the CEO of DecisionWise, which for over two decades has advised organizations across the globe on the employee experience. As a consultant, industrial-organizational psychologist, researcher, and business executive, Maylett's work has been published in numerous academic and business publications as well as the bestselling books *The Employee Experience: How to Attract Talent, Retain Top Performers, and Drive Results* (2017) and *Engagement MAGIC: Five Keys for Engaging People, Leaders, and Organizations* (2019). He holds a doctorate in organizational change from Pepperdine University and an MBA from Brigham Young University, where he also teaches in BYU's Marriott School of Business and University Honors programs.

Tim Vandehey is a journalist, columnist, and *New York Times* bestselling ghostwriter of more than sixty-five nonfiction books in genres such as business, finance, advice, outdoor adventure, religion, memoir, parenting, and health. His work has been featured in

Fast Company, Inc., *Forbes*, and *Entrepreneur*, and his ghostwritten books have been published by major houses, including Harper-Collins, Simon & Schuster, Hachette, Wiley, St. Martin's Press, and MIT Press. Vandehey's work has also garnered numerous awards, including multiple Axiom Business Book Awards and Independent Publisher book awards. He holds a bachelor's degree in English from California State University, Fullerton.

For more information, self-assessments, and additional valuable resources, visit:

SWIPETHEBOOK.COM

Contact Us

Tracy
🐦 @tracymaylett
in linkedin.com/in/tracymaylett

Tim
in linkedin.com/in/tvandehey

Index

A

Achor, Shawn, 81
adaptation, 209–212
    intentional, 211
    voluntary, 211
adjustment, 209–212
advancement, in workplace, 81
Adventures of Buckaroo Banzai, The,
    86
Age of the Employee, 74, 77, 86
akrasia, 197
Allen, David, 13
Alvin, Amelia, 33, 35
Amabile, Teresa, 216
Amazon, 128
ambiguity, 126–129
    deficit, 127–129
    and technology, 127–128
American Automobile Association,
    178
American Psychological Association,
    189
"American Regret Project," 158

Anna Karenina (Tolstoy), 38
anticipatory stress, 150
Aristotle, 197
attention, 164–167, 171, 173–176,
    183–186
    asymmetry, 155, 158
    limits of, 178–180
    mastering, 190–200
    multitasking, 183–190
augmented reality, 125
autonomy
    in MAGIC, 96
    and Strong Goals, 106
avoidance, 151

B

babies, and swiping movements, 5–6
Ballmer, Steve, 225
Bandura, Albert, 149–150
Barton, William, 117
Bastian, Brock, 54, 140
Baty, Chris, 3–4
Baumeister, Roy, 139

behavior
    and adaptation, 209
    change and technology,
      121–123
    and smartphone, 120
Belafonte, Harry, 26
Bezos, Jeff, 103
bias, 69–70, 148
    optimism, 109
    unconscious, 8
Biles, Simone, 28–29
BlackBerry, 120
Blink (Gladwell), 196
Blockbuster, 22–23
Bonga, Isaac, 161
brain. *See* human brain
Branson, Richard, 103
Brislane, Niche, 102
Brooks, Garth, 139
Brown, Brené, 60
Bryson, Bill, 114
Bumble, 6–7
bypassing, and Swiping, 29–30

C

Calhoun, Lawrence, 55
Carr, Nicholas, 126–127
catalytic questions, 213
Catchings, Cynthia, 65–66
"Cat's in the Cradle," 60
celebrities, 5–6
Chabris, Christopher, 175, 177
Chapin, Harry, 60
Christakis, Nicholas A., 98
chronic procrastinators, 20
Cinder (Meyer), 4
Click, 53, 138, 180
cognitive neuroscience, 174
comfort zone, 150–152
completion

creating habit of, 217–218
    as sense of accomplishment,
      215–217
connection, in MAGIC, 98
Coraci, Frank, 53
Covey, Stephen, 204–205
COVID-19 pandemic, 69, 75, 86
Crandell, Todd, 15, 17
creating space, 218–219
Credit Karma, 63
Crowhurst, Donald, 112–113
Csíkszentmihályi, Mihály, 108
curation, defined, 131

D

"Dance, The" (song), 139
Darwin Elevator, The (Hough), 4
decimation, 77
DecisionWise, 20, 82, 85, 94
discomfort. *See also* mental discom-
    fort
    accept, 207–208
    appreciate, 207–208
    and growth, 208
disengagement, employees, 80
    MAGIC, 94–100
    reasons for, 87–88
    self-sabotage, 91–94
disengagement, 73–100
    as self-defense, 61
    temporary, 208
Disillusionment Swipe, 39–40
*Distracted Mind: Ancient Brains in a
    High-Tech World, The* (Gazzaley
    and Rosen), 163, 184
distraction
    defined, 169–170
    and human brain, 166–168
    ill effects of, 170
    social media as, 142–143

and stimuli filtering, 180
and technology, 134–135
of university students, 141–144
Drenner, Monte, 56
Duckworth, Angela, 23, 144
Dunning, David, 112
Dunning-Kruger effect, 112

E

ease of circumstance, and smartphone, 132–133
ease of execution, and smartphone, 132
ego, 149
Ego Swipe, 42
Ellis, Stanley G., 27–28
Emerson, Ralph Waldo, 198
emotional regulation, and technology, 64
emotions, 220–221
empathy
    deficit, 68
    disincentivized, 70
    and Swiping, 68–70
Employee Experience, The (Wride), 74–75
employees, 89. *See also* disengagement, employees; engagement, employees
    quitting, 84–86
    Swiping, 84–86, 88–90
engagement, employees, 78–81
    and advancement, 81
    happiness, 80–81
    and health, 80
    and home life, 81
    importance of, 82–84
    and pay, 81
    and productivity, 81
Engagement MAGIC (Maylett), 87

Ennui Swipe, 40
Enron, 22
escapism, 151
Eurich, Tasha, 204
evaluation, and Swipe, 225–226
evidence-based management, 225
experiences
    employee, 77, 97
    intense, 55
    negative, 54, 139–140
    peak experiences, 140
    positive, 139–140
    uncomfortable, 208
explicit memory, 194
exposure therapy, 125

F

Facebook, 62
"fail forward fast" doctrine, 36
family bonds, and swiping, 59–61
Fangirl (Rowell), 4
Faruz, Aviad, 201–202
"fast-twitch" athletes, 193
fatalism, 30
Ferguson, Scott, 122
Ferrari, Joseph, 20
Finder, 20
flake, 58
Fogg, B. J., 218
FOMO (fear of missing out), 62–63
Forbes, 36
Fowler, James H., 98
Frankl, Viktor, 205
Frederickson, Jon, 48
Freud, Sigmund, 149
fustuarium, 76

G

García, Joaquín, 73–74
Gates, Bill, 225
Gazzaley, Adam, 163, 172, 183–184
ghosting, 84
Gilbert, Daniel, 143
Gladwell, Malcolm, 196–197
Google, 5, 127
Google Maps, 6
Gordon, Sherri, 63
Grant, Adam, 88
Great Resignation, 70, 75, 84, 86, 95, 99–100
Greener Grass Swipe, 40–41
Gregersen, Hal, 213–214, 219
Grit: The Power of Passion and Perseverance (Duckworth), 24, 144
growth, in MAGIC, 96–97
Gruen, Sara, 4
Guardian, 73–74

H

habituation, 207
Hall, Leanne, 208
Halo Infinite, 190
hands, and engagement, 79
Hanson, Veronica, 67
happiness
    employee engagement, 80–81
    and positive experiences, 139–140
Happiness Advantage, The (Achor), 81
Harding, Samantha, 34–35
Harvard Business Review, 75
Harvard Youth Poll, 65
health
    and employee engagement, 80
    mental, 63–68

and placebo effect, 43
heart, and engagement, 79
Hess, Daniel, 211
home life, and employee engagement, 81
Homer, 169
Hough, Jason, 4
Howey, Hugh, 4
"How Smartphones Hijack Our Minds," 126–127
Hugo, Victor, 41
human brain
    and body, 161–163
    and distraction, 166–168
    and information gathering, 173
    neurons in, 162
    processing and storage capacity of, 162
human cost of Swipe, 53–71
Hurricane Sandy, 69

I

id, 149
impact, in MAGIC, 97–98
implicit memory, 194
impostor syndrome, 50
Impostor Syndrome Swipe, 42
inattentional blindness, 175, 177
inciting incident, 202
information filtering, 173–174
information foraging, 172–173
Inspector Javert Swipe, 41
Instagram, 62, 155
intellectual atrophy, 127
intense experiences, 55
intention-action gap, 152
intentional adaptation, 211
Intimidation Swipe, 39
iPhone, 6, 120, 142–143

J

James, William, 170
Jha, Amishi P., 165–168
"Job Swipe," 75
Jobvite, 85
Jordan, Michael, 165
Journal of Positive Psychology, 140
Journal of the American Medical Association, 47

K

Kabat-Zinn, Jon, 86
Kader, Ruhul, 104
Kafka on the Shore (Murakami), 212
Kahneman, Daniel, 144–145
Kander, Jason, 29
Kelly, Patrick, 101
Killingsworth, Matthew, 143
Kramer, Steve, 216
Kruger, Justin, 112

L

LaVine, Zach, 161
learned helplessness, 65
legatus, 76, 78
Lennon, John, 181
Les Misérables (Hugo), 41
lies, 48–51
Lies We Tell Ourselves: How to Face the Truth, Accept Yourself, and Create a Better Life, The (Frederickson), 48
Light Phone II, 119–120
Limitless, 163
load theory, 174–175
Locke, Edwin, 106
long-term memory, 194
Lucy, 163

M

MAGIC, 82, 94–100
managers, 89
Marius, Gaius, 76
Markkanen, Lauri, 161
Maslow, Abraham, 140
mastery, 193–197, 199
Match.com, 123
Matchmaker, 123
Material Design system (Google), 5
McCormack, Chris "Macca," 18–19
meaning, in MAGIC, 95–96
memory, 163, 194–195, 223
    working, 190–192, 199
mental discomfort, 150–151. *See also* discomfort
    positive psychological reasons for Swipe, 151
mental health
    and screen time, 156
    and smartphones, 157
    and Swipe, 63–68
Mental Health Has Bigger Challenges Than Stigma report, 66
Mental Health Million Project, 66
Meta (Facebook), 87
Meyer, Marissa, 4
Miller, Daniel, 121
mind. *See also* human brain
    and attention, 171
    and body, 161–163
    described, 170–171
    in engagement, 79
mobile phone. *See also* smartphone
    as communication tool, 120
Mochon, Daniel, 216
Morgenstern, Erin, 4
Morin, Amy, 64
motivation, 25–26, 66–67, 134–135
Motorola Razr, 120
multitasking, 183–184

ineffectiveness of, 186–187
research on, 184–186
vs. task switching, 186–189
Murakami, Haruki, 212
Murphy, Sean, 54, 140
Musk, Elon, 103

N

Nadella, Satya, 225
narrative identity perspective, 55
Nass, Cliff, 184
National Geographic, 122
National Institutes of Health, 37
National Novel Writing Month
    (NaNoWriMo), 3–4, 17, 40
negative experiences, 54, 139–140
Netflix, 22–23
neuroplasticity, 198
new-car paradox, 171
New York Times, 63
Niessen, Cornelia, 85
Night Circus, The (Morgenstern), 4

O

Oculus Rift, 125
Odyssey (Homer), 169
OkCupid, 123
optimism bias, 109
organizations, 9, 12, 22, 37, 74,
    77–78, 83, 85–86, 89, 226
Outliers (Gladwell), 197

P

page-one energy, 17–19, 25–26, 108
Pallardy, Richard, 6
PalmPilot, 120
"passive sabotage," 90

Pathak, Shirani, 92
pay, and employee engagement, 81
peak experiences, 140
Penberthy, J. Kim, 159
Phelps, Michael, 101
Pink, Daniel, 158–160
Pinterest, 106
placebo effect, 43
Plato, 197
pleasure-pain principle, 149
Plenty of Fish, 123
positive experiences
    and happiness, 139–140
    and meaningful life, 140
posttraumatic growth, 55
Power of Regret, The (Pink), 158–160
pre-swipe warning signs, 25–27
procedural learning, 194–195
procedural memory, 194
procrastination, 20, 103–104
productivity, and employee engage-
    ment, 81
Progress Principle, The (Amabile and
    Kramer), 216
Psychology Today, 63
Pychyl, Tim, 103–104

Q

Questions Are the Answer (Gregers-
    en), 213
quitting and Swiping, 84–86

R

Racing for Recovery, 15–16
Radically Open Dialectical Behavior
    Therapy (RODBT), 222
reality, 125
Reddit, 59

reflection, 204–207, 212–214
regret, 7, 46, 48, 50, 117–118,
    158–160
"regrettable omissions," 24
*Rethinking Failure: A Short Guide
    to Living an Entrepreneurial Life*
    (Kader), 104
reticular activating system (RAS),
    171
Rosen, Larry, 163, 172, 184
Rowell, Rainbow, 4
Rowling, J. K., 39
Rozin, Paul, 54
Ruiz, Rosie, 36

S

sabotage, 88–89
    passive, 90
    self-, 91–94
    workplace, 92–93
Sandler, Adam, 53, 138–139, 141,
    180
Saunders, Allen, 181
Schroeder, Jenna, 161–162, 164
Scientific American, 68
selectivity, 174
self-control, 242n9
self-defense, disengagement as, 61
self-efficacy, 30, 106, 114, 118, 131,
    134, 149–150
self-inquiry, 222–223
self-sabotage, 91–94
Seligman, Martin, 65
*Seven Habits of Highly Effective Peo-
    ple, The* (Covey), 204
Sharot, Tali, 109
Shimanoff, Susan, 159
Simons, Daniel, 175, 177
Simple Sabotage Field Manual, The,
    89

skepticism, 44–45
Skinner, B. F., 126
smartphone
    and alternate realities, 121
    augmented reality applications
        on, 125
    and behavior, 120
    dependency, 120
    and ease of circumstance,
        132–133
    and ease of execution, 132
    and mental health, 157
social media, 142–143
Socrates, 197
"Some Key Differences Between a
    Happy Life and Meaningful Life,"
    139
Sons, Meike, 85
sour-grape effect, 50
Spinoza, Baruch, 74
spirit, and engagement, 79
SportsCenter, 162
stakes fallacy, 59
stasis, 30
storyteller's conceit, 55
Sunday Times Golden Globe Race,
    112
supervisors, 89
Swipe/Swiping, 33–51, 218–222
    as anti-master, 198–200
    and death of empathy, 68–70
    Disillusionment, 39–40
    and distraction, 180–181
    Ego, 42
    Ennui, 40
    and family bonds, 59–61
    and FOMO, 62–63
    Greener Grass, 40–41
    how not to, 153–154, 223–224
    human cost of, 53–71
    Impostor Syndrome, 42

Inspector Javert, 41
intimidation, 39
and mental health, 63–68
and perception of others, 56–58
positive about, 70–71
positive psychological reasons
for, 151
and quitting, 84–86
in romantic partners, 60
science of failure, 35–38
and self-inquiry, 222–223
taxonomy of, 38–43
Trapped Animal, 42–43
universal, 19–23
Swipe-switch, 153–154
Swipe Wants, 107
System One thinking, 145–148, 160
as id, 149
and mental discomfort, 151
and Swipe, 148–149, 154–158
System Two thinking, 145–148, 160
and Swipe, 148–149

T

"Tantrums, Toddlers, and Technology," 64
tapping out, 27–31
task switching
defined, 188
vs. multitasking, 186–189
taxonomy of Swipes, 38–43
technology
and ambiguity, 127–128
and behavior change, 121–123
and distraction, 134–135
and emotional regulation, 64
and motivation, 134–135
reduce use in daily life,
131–132
Tedeschi, Richard, 55

teenagers and Swiping, 5–6
Teignmouth Electron, 112–113
telephone, 89–90
This Old House, 25
Thoreau, Henry David, 215
Tinder, 6
and swipe gesture, 123–125,
126
techno courtship, 124
Tinder Effect, 124
Todorov, Alex, 124
Tolkien, J. R. R., 39
Tolstoy, Leo, 38
transportation, 90
Trapped Animal Swipe, 42–43
Two Minds, 144–148

U

unhappiness, formula for, 23–24
University College London, 121
University of Texas, 120
US National Highway Traffic Safety
Administration, 170

V

value-action gap, 152
virtual reality, 125
virtue signaling, 69
voluntary adaptation, 211
VUCA (volatility, uncertainty, complexity, and ambiguity), 56

W

Walk in the Woods, A (Bryson), 114
Wall Street Journal, 126
Wang, Dashun, 37
Ward, Adrian, 120

Water for Elephants (Gruen), 4
Weak Wants, 106–108
whiteboards, 191–192
Williams, Lauren, 161
Willis Towers Watson, 21
Winfrey, Oprah, 103
Wolfe, Thomas, 46
Wool (Howey), 4
working memory, 190–192
workplace
    ghosting, 84
    "honeymoon period," 85
    sabotage, 92–93
Wride, Matthew, 74

Y

Yen, Brian, 37

Z

Zeigarnik effect, 24